CELTIC
SCOTLAND

HJ

for my mother

CELTIC
SCOTLAND

IAN ARMIT

B. T. Batsford Ltd / Historic Scotland

© Ian Armit 1997
First published 1997

Typeset by Bernard Cavender Design & Greenwood Graphics Publishing
and printed by The Bath Press, Bath

Published by B. T. Batsford Ltd
583 Fulham Road, London SW6 5BY

A CIP catalogue record for this book is
available from the British Library.

ISBN 0 7134 7538 2(limp)
0 7134 7537 4(cased)

(*Front cover*) Dun Carloway, Lewis, in its landscape setting
(*Back cover*) The Stichill collar, a fine example of Early
Celtic art, found in Roxburghshire

Contents

Illustrations

Colour plates

Acknowledgements

This book is an inevitably personal exploration of an important but under-studied period of Scottish history. As such, it cannot hope to be definitive. Indeed, almost all new excavations of any size conspire to undermine our carefully assembled frameworks and theories. In such a fast-moving field of study I can only hope to achieve a snapshot of our understanding as it is in 1997.

The ideas presented here are founded on the work of numerous scholars and I cannot stress too much the debt that is owed to their efforts. There is no scope in a work of this kind to list the academic books and papers that form the foundation of our present understanding, but the bibliographies of the general works cited at the end of this book, or a perusal of the pages of the *Proceedings of the Society of Antiquaries of Scotland*, will give some idea.

I would like to thank Dr David Breeze for encouraging me to write this book, and for his sound advice and careful editing thereafter. I am also grateful to those who read and commented upon earlier drafts: Dr Jane Conroy, Trevor Cowie, Dr Noel Fojut, Jackie Henrie, Catriona Leask, Dr Ian Ralston and Professor John Waddell.

Several colleagues kindly allowed reference to their work in advance of publication, including Patrick Ashmore, Dr Anne Crone, Steve Dockrill, Dr Sally Foster, Dr Jane Conroy, Dr Stephen Driscoll, Andrew Dunwell, Richard Hingley, John Hope, Fraser Hunter, Dr Ian Ralston, Richard Strachan and Professor John Waddell. Patrick Ashmore provided assistance with radiocarbon dates throughout. Staff of the Royal Commission on the Ancient and Historical Monuments of Scotland assisted throughout and I would particularly like to thank Marilyn Brown, Dr Gordon Maxwell, Lesley Fergusson, and Roger Mercer for their help. Alan Braby brought the evidence of excavation to life with his reconstruction drawings, and also drew all of the other original illustrations.

The author and publisher would also like to thank the following for permission to reproduce illustrations: The Trustees of the National Museum of Scotland (8, 26, 51–2, 55, 57, 61, 75, colour plates 5, 10–12, 15), the Royal Commission on the Ancient and Historical Monuments of Scotland (10, 13, 25, 31b, 32–4, 36–7, 41, 44–5, 48–9, 64, 66, 70–2, 76–8, colour plates 6, 7), the Danish National Museum (62), Fife Council (56), Dr David Breeze (1, 73, colour plate 13), and Historic Scotland (6, 17, 18, 29, 31a, 60, 63, 74, colour plates 1–4, 8, 9, 14). Illus. 60 was drawn by Marion O'Neill and is reproduced by permission of The Trustees of the National Museum of Scotland. The photograph of the author is by Graeme Stuart.

1
Celtic Scotland?

By rights this book should probably be called 'Celtic Scotland?' The question mark is apposite in more than one sense. First, the suggestion that Scotland, in the period from around 1000 BC to around AD 500, was the preserve of Celts is unlikely to be uniformly welcomed. Second, even if such a proposition were to be accepted, this 'Celticness' would be hard to define.

It is no surprise that modern British archaeologists generally recoil from the term 'Celtic'. Its vagueness and association with dewy-eyed mysticism are anathema to many who prefer to stick to the material facts of prehistory. It is no easy matter to define what we mean by 'Celtic', particularly in the prehistoric past. Speakers of Celtic languages, for example, may not have corresponded exactly with the makers of what we call Celtic art, and none of these people need have thought of themselves as Celts or adhered to any common culture or identity. Yet, to ignore the commonalities of language, material culture and social development across Europe in the Later Bronze Age and Iron Age would leave us with an insular and limited perspective on the nation's past. The Celts, then, must be faced.

As we approach the end of the millennium, our prehistoric heritage is being dusted down as a symbol of the new unified Europe. European states have cooperated, through the Council of Europe, for example, in launching a celebration of the Bronze Age, with accompanying literature that vigorously promotes the vision of a shared

destiny based on a shared heritage, in which the Celts play a significant part.

The predecessors of most present European states, however, had little time for the Celts. All over Europe, Celtic-speaking cultures were more or less eclipsed, first by the Roman empire, and subsequently, as in England, by Germanic-speaking societies (1). Celtic-speaking peoples survived on the margins of Europe, for example in Brittany and Cornwall (2), but only in Ireland and Gaelic Scotland did they retain power long enough to form recognizable medieval states, and only in Ireland did a Celtic state survive into modern times.

Scotland lost its last truly Celtic king with the death of MacBeth in AD 1057. His subsequent vilification by increasingly anglicized successors reflects the distaste for Gaelic culture evident in lowland Scottish culture through much of its history. Yet the early kingdoms that had coalesced into the Scottish state a few centuries earlier (the Scots, Picts and Britons) were all essentially Celtic, with their roots in the Europe-wide cultural traditions of the Iron Age.

A whole range of questions is bound up with the study of this 'Celticness'. How did Scotland acquire a Celtic-speaking population – was it by immigration, conquest or gradual cultural mutation? What relationship, if any, did the Bronze and Iron Age tribes of Scotland have with other nominally Celtic peoples across Europe? Was there an awareness of any shared

1 The war-leader Calgacus addresses the Scottish tribes before the battle of Mons Graupius. A traditional Celtic image.

ethnicity or culture in the Scottish Iron Age and, if so, did this contribute to the emergence of the Early Historic kingdoms of the Scots, Picts and Britons? With the potentially volatile role of ethnicity having recently been brought sharply into focus in Europe, archaeologists are again taking an interest in such issues.

2 Celtic languages are traditionally divided into two groups: Q-Celtic, the more linguistically conservative form, comprising Irish and Scots Gaelic, and Manx, and P-Celtic, in which the archaic 'qu' and 'k' sounds had been replaced by a 'p' sound, comprising Welsh, Cornish and Breton. Other known Celtic languages – Gaulish, Brittonic, Cumbric, Pictish, Lepontic and Celtiberian – were uniformly extinct before AD 800.

Who were the Celts? ...

Greek and Roman references to the Celts occur from around the sixth century BC, and in 390 BC they were encountered uncomfortably close at hand when Celtic war-bands sacked Rome itself as well as rampaging through Greece and establishing control over parts of Anatolia. Following the Roman annexation of northern Italy and much of Mediterranean France from around 200–120 BC, classical writers were able to extend their first-hand knowledge of the Celts under rather more controlled conditions. Posidonius, who became, via later copyists, the source of much of our knowledge of the historical Celts, may have travelled in Celtic Gaul at around this time (3).

There was, however, little consistency among the classical authors. The early Greek sources ascribe various territories in western Europe, particularly parts of France and Spain, to a people known to them as the Celts ('Keltoi' in Greek). Later writers tend to be rather more specific: Caesar, writing in the first century BC, for example, states that the Celtae (or 'Galli' in Latin) were one of three peoples occupying the southern and central parts of what is now France. Strabo, writing at around the same time, suggests that it was the proximity of these Celtae to the Greek colony of Massilia (modern Marseilles), founded around 600 BC, that had led to their name being applied generically to the peoples of the region. Thus, if there ever was a prehistoric people who called themselves by a name resembling Celtae or Keltoi, they were probably restricted to a relatively small area of south and central France.

By contrast, numerous closely related languages, which have long since been classed together as Celtic, are attested over substantial areas of northern and western Europe (see 2). Thus, however inappropriate the name Celtic might be in its wider application, people in these areas of Europe formed a recognizable linguistic, if not cultural, group.

Unlike the Romans or Greeks, who were fully conscious of their own identity and culture, there is no evidence that there was, in the pre-Roman period, any sense of kinship or ethnicity among the groups of people who spoke what we would now regard as Celtic languages. Celtic culture was in a sense constructed (like that of the understandably less fashionable Aryans) by continental scholars in the latter half of the nineteenth century. Indeed, no classical author ever referred to the British tribes as Celts: that equation was made in more recent centuries by the extrapolation of linguistic and artefactual evidence.

It was during the nineteenth century that the chronological skeleton of Celtic culture in Europe was formed, much of it based on two sites that lent their names to the two major and successive periods of the European Later Bronze Age and Iron Age: Hallstatt in Austria, a vast

13

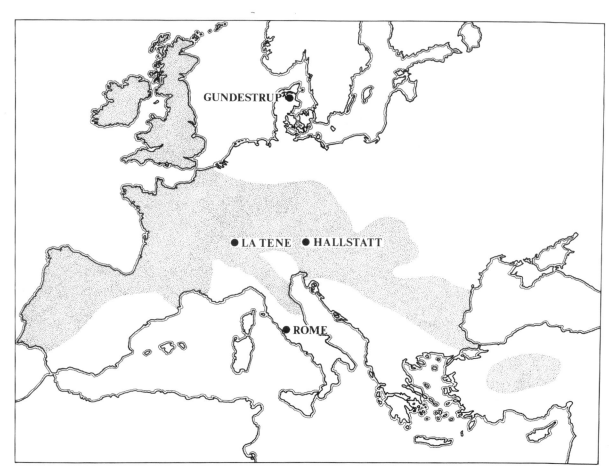

3 At its height, around 200 BC, 'Celtic culture', as measured by the occurrence of certain artefact types and art styles, spread across much of Europe and into Anatolia.

cemetery, and La Tène in Switzerland, where masses of decorative metalwork and other objects were recovered from the drained waters of Lake Neuchâtel. It was the study of artefacts from those sites that enabled the construction of the first detailed chronologies for the European Later Bronze Age and Iron Age.

The creation of these archaeological cultures, Hallstatt and La Tène, seemed to have produced the material remains of the Celtic peoples known to the Greeks and Romans. Until relatively recently, archaeologists were content to equate regular groupings of material remains, or cultures, with prehistoric peoples. Thus the historical Celts, Hallstatt and La Tène artefacts and art styles, and Celtic languages could all be bundled together to recreate a lost European culture.

However, this culture-history approach to archaeology can be very misleading. Hallstatt and La Tène material culture and decoration may have penetrated vast areas of Europe but they fail to correspond to any regular changes in settlement, burial or other aspects of local culture. What has often been seen as the expansion of a Celtic people need have been little more than the spread of art styles and fashions. There is no necessary or even likely connection between Hallstatt and La Tène artefacts and Celtic languages, which probably had a rather wider social and geographical currency: Celtic-speakers in parts of Ireland, Spain and Portugal, for example, seem to have largely eschewed La Tène material. While people who used La Tène items were most probably Celtic-speakers, not all Celtic-speakers used La Tène items.

For the purposes of this book, the term 'Celt' will be restricted to speakers of Celtic languages.

... and when?

The terms 'Stone Age', 'Bronze Age' and 'Iron Age' were introduced by Danish scholars in the nineteenth century primarily as a means of ordering museum collections. While these classifications have long outlived their usefulness, the 'Iron Age' survives as archaeological shorthand for the period from around 700 BC, when iron was first introduced into Britain, while the preceding period is still referred to as the Later Bronze Age. In England, the Iron Age ends with the Claudian invasion in AD 43, but in Scotland it carries on to merge imperceptibly with what is conventionally known as the Early Historic period in the middle of the first millennium AD (4).

In this book I will, without further justification, describe the period from around 1200 to 700 BC as the Later Bronze Age, 700 BC until AD 500 as the Iron Age, and AD 500 onwards as the Early Historic period. Parts of the country saw varying degrees of Roman interference from the AD 80s to the fourth century AD, and I shall uncritically, from time to time, call this the period of Roman influence. It is important to remember, however, that all of these start and end dates are nothing more than a convenient shorthand.

An overview

It is hard for any archaeologist to avoid becoming embroiled in the detail of broch architecture, hillfort morphology or other such absorbing minutiae. The wealth of such data combined with the absence of wide-ranging explanatory frameworks probably explains why, despite a long and honourable tradition of study, this is the first general book to be written about this period of Scotland's history since Joseph Anderson's *Scotland in Pagan Times: The Iron Age*, in 1883. In the chapters which follow I will attempt to bring together the archaeological evidence for society in Scotland

between around 1000 BC–AD 500, in the light of some of the questions relating to Celtic culture and identity. Inevitably, much of the material demands discussion at the local or regional scale, but the relationship to wider developments in Europe will be a recurrent theme.

It is worth stating at the outset some basic features of the period. First, this was a time when enormous effort was put into the construction of homes of one sort or another. At some times and in some places these took the form of substantial roundhouses of timber or stone, at others, massive forts or artificial islet dwellings, all displaying marked regional variation (5). Secondly, although life appears to have been steeped in ritual, formal burials are exceedingly rare. Thirdly, this period saw the intensive clearance of forest from much of Scotland and the establishment of thriving farming economies. Fourthly, by the end of the period, recognizable states were emerging from the hazily defined petty kingdoms and tribes of the pre-Roman period.

Against this background, numerous technological innovations were adopted, including the use of iron for tools and weapons, and the rotary quern for grinding grain. During the latter centuries of the period, the Roman army came and went, the extent and nature of its impact remaining a matter of considerable debate. At various times, elaborate bronze artefacts, Celtic (or La Tène) art, Celtic personal names, tribal names and place-names, and the emergence of Celtic-speaking kingdoms in the post-Roman centuries, all link Scotland to the wider European scene.

Equally important, however, is an understanding of two features that do not characterize the period. First, society from the Later Bronze Age to the Early Historic periods was far from static. It is characterized by marked changes over time and between different parts of the country. Secondly, change was not unilinear, that is, there was no inexorable march of progress towards increased centralization or

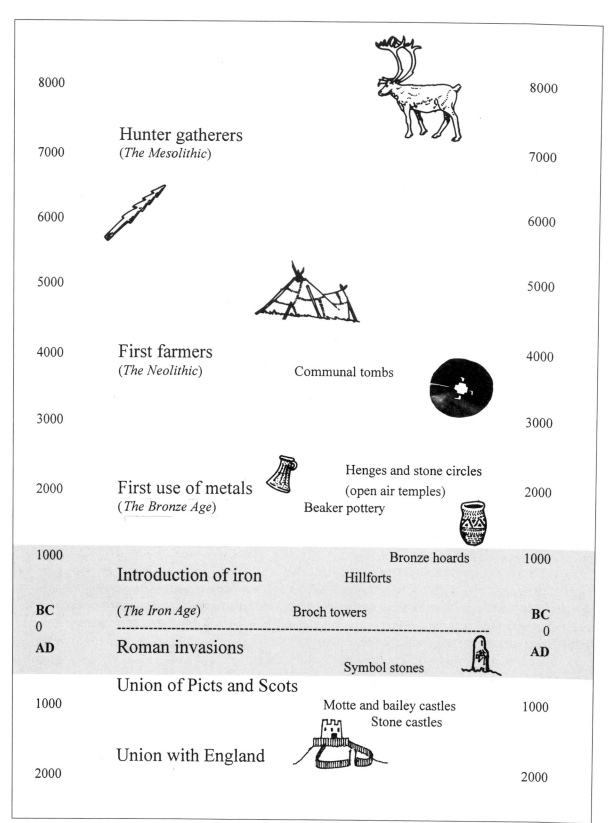

8000 — 8000

Hunter gatherers
(*The Mesolithic*)

7000 — 7000

6000 — 6000

5000 — 5000

4000 — 4000

First farmers
(*The Neolithic*)   Communal tombs

3000 — 3000

Henges and stone circles
(open air temples)

2000 —   First use of metals   2000
(*The Bronze Age*)   Beaker pottery

1000 —   Bronze hoards   1000
Introduction of iron   Hillforts

BC   (*The Iron Age*)   Broch towers   BC
0   0
AD   Roman invasions   AD

Symbol stones

Union of Picts and Scots

1000 —   Motte and bailey castles   1000
Stone castles

Union with England

2000 — 2000

4 People have lived in Scotland since at least 7500 BC, initially on plant and animal foods gathered and hunted from the land and sea. From around 4000 BC people began to adopt agriculture and build great burial and ritual monuments. Forests began to be cleared as populations grew. New technologies like pottery and, much later, bronze, augmented stone, wood, bone and other naturally occurring materials. So, by the start of our period, around 1000 BC, Scotland was already a settled land, its landscape heavily altered by over 2000 years of agriculture and forest clearance and littered with overgrown and decaying tombs, stone circles and ritual enclosures.

coherence. Instead there appear to have been alternating periods of stability and unrest, political control and fragmentation. Indeed, the Later Bronze Age may have been a time when rulers were more powerful and exchange networks more widespread than at the time of the Roman invasions some eight centuries later. Virtually every aspect of the archaeological evidence conspires to deny any view of an easily definable, timeless Celtic past.

A cautionary note on dating

In the chapters which follow, the chronology of archaeological sites and periods will be based substantially on radiocarbon dating, except for occasional dates from documents in the Roman period and later, and extrapolations to undated and unexcavated sites. Dates will be quoted in 'calendar' years BC and AD using the methods available as of 1997, and generally without discussion of such important variables as sample material or statistical standard deviation. Radiocarbon dates for the period are sparse and prone to periodically wild error, but they are, for now, the best guide we have. The chronology of the period remains very weakly established and my attempt to construct a narrative is inevitably highly provisional.

5 The natural environment and physical geography of Scotland have always influenced the societies who have lived here. In the period from around 1000 BC to AD 500 this regionalism is especially marked. For example, the fragmented landscapes of the north and west played a part in the development of small dispersed settlements in contrast to the large hillforts of the more open landscapes to the south and east. But, as we shall see, simple environmental factors are insufficient to explain the wealth and diversity of this period of Scottish prehistory.

2
Ancestral lands

Celtic origins

'But where did they come from?' is a favourite question of visitors to archaeological excavations. The image of a prehistoric past in which tribes or peoples engaged in a perpetual flux of invasion, colonization and displacement remains firmly fixed in the popular consciousness. Yet this perception reflects a mode of archaeological thought belonging to the earlier part of this century. Today's explanations, which lay more stress on the development of indigenous peoples, with perhaps only occasional population movements, have singularly failed to capture the public imagination.

As one of the more colourful components of the remoter British past, the origins of the Celts excite more curiosity than most. So where and when did the Celts first emerge? One answer is that they originated in the minds of the nineteenth-century antiquarians who first assembled prehistoric Celtic 'culture' from the fragments of archaeological, linguistic and art-historical knowledge available to them. But this, however tempting, is unsatisfactory. There was a Celtic milieu in Iron Age Europe, comprising language, art and artefacts, which corresponds, albeit inexactly, with the peoples grouped together by the Romans and Greeks as Celts, Gauls, Britons and Caledonians. The origins of this Celtic world lie in the Europe of the Later Bronze Age, particularly the period from around 1200 to 700 BC, and it is to the cultural changes taking place in this period that we must look if we are to understand the 'origins of the Celts'.

The end of the old religions

The Later Bronze Age in Britain and Ireland saw the culmination of a period of momentous social change. The great monuments of the Neolithic period, the stone circles, henges and processional cursus monuments, had fallen into apparent disuse (these monuments and the communities who built them are described in Patrick Ashmore's book *Neolithic and Bronze Age Scotland* in this series) and the communal graves of the early farming communities had been superseded by the elaborate tombs of prominent individuals.

The Neolithic period in Britain was devoid of signs of secular kings or high chiefs; instead, the highest status seems to have belonged to priests who officiated rites of communal ritual at which dispersed communities periodically came together. Sites like Calanais (or Callanish) in Lewis, Cairnpapple in West Lothian and the Ring of Brodgar in Orkney were the Scottish equivalents of Stonehenge and Avebury in southern England (**6**).

However, from around 2000 BC these communal monuments underwent dramatic transformations. At Cairnpapple the stone circle was dismantled and the stones were re-used to build a cairn housing the remains a single individual. Aside from the hi-jacking of earlier monuments, many new single graves were built

as the glorification of the individual, and his or her descendants became the focus of monument building. By the Later Bronze Age, formal monuments had been all but abandoned and links with the Neolithic past severed.

It seems that the Neolithic theocracy had been gradually replaced by a secular aristocracy where religious specialists played only a supporting role. It has been suggested that there had also been a change in the nature of the gods that were most venerated, from sky gods, worshipped at Calanais and Stonehenge, whose

6 The main stone setting at Calanais in Lewis was one of the finest expressions of the 'old order' of the Neolithic and was probably associated with celestial or lunar deities. Such communal monuments would have formed a focus for acts of worship and social contacts between groups of people who perhaps seldom came into direct contact in the course of their daily lives. The similarities between large ritual centres in different parts of Britain suggests that there were widespread contacts, but there is no sign of the secular chiefs that we see manifested through rich burials and extravagant sacrificial hoards during the Bronze Age.

moods and actions were encoded in the sun, moon and stars, to underworld or earth gods more akin to those that emerge centuries later as the pagan Celtic pantheon: gods whose activities reflected the 'heroic' ideologies of the Celtic aristocracy.

Networks of exchange

Major social changes also ushered in the Later Bronze Age on the Continent. The period after 1200 BC is characterized in many parts of Central and Mediterranean Europe by the fall and fragmentation of long-established powers, such as the Mycenaean civilization in Greece and the Hittite Empire in Anatolia. Smaller social units, dominated by warrior groups based in fortified settlements, came to the fore, even in Greece and the islands of the eastern Mediterranean where the proto-urban civilizations based around the Mycenaean and Minoan palaces had earlier held sway. The resultant militaristic and fragmented social system is graphically portrayed in Homer's *Iliad* and *Odyssey*.

In this 'heroic age', from around 1200 to 700 BC, a series of overlapping exchange networks seem to have facilitated the spread of ideas from one end of Europe to the other. One such zone of communication stretched across the north German plain and southern Scandinavia, while another encompassed Britain, Ireland, and extended down the Atlantic coast to southern Spain. Different regions had their own range of specialisms. Ireland was a centre for the production of fine bronze and goldwork, including a range of dress fasteners and personal jewellery (7). Another fine bronze-working tradition was centred in Denmark where specialized ritual items supplemented more mundane objects.

The manufacture of bronze made some degree of exchange inevitable, since its raw materials, copper and tin, rarely occur close together. Pack animals, carts and boats would have become ever more important in the cultural and economic lives of communities

7 Some Bronze Age artefact types circulated over wide areas. These were made for the upper echelons of Bronze Age society who had a voracious appetite for exotic and elaborate items. But what were the mechanics of this circulation? Each generation of archaeologists has had its own answers. Once, colonization and invasion were the favoured mechanisms of cultural spread. Later archaeologists favoured a proto-free market, in which communities engaged in rather more civil forms of barter and exchange. However, nowadays, most archaeologists interpret this phenomenon as the result of widespread social rather than economic bargaining between elites, in which goods travelled as gifts associated with alliances, marriages and tribute.

across Europe as land, sea and riverine routes were explored and exploited. But although metal goods are the most archaeologically visible remnants of these networks, numerous other goods would also have been exchanged. Furs, exotic foods, slaves, animals, amber, shale and other commodities would have travelled the same pathways, as, of course, would the traders themselves. With them would have spread technical knowledge, cultural ideas, myths and stories and, as we shall see below, languages.

A 1994 publication by the Council of Europe goes so far as to describe Bronze Age Europe as 'a shifting mosaic of regional identities bound closer by a common interest in trade and enterprise'. This probably overstates the case, implying commercial attitudes and market economies more characteristic of modern capitalist societies than the kin-based and largely rural communities of the Bronze Age. Rather than trade we should think of these networks as promoting reciprocal exchange, where social ties and obligations such as gift-giving, bride-wealth, sacrifice and the conspicuous display of wealth created demand for exotic goods and elaborate artefacts.

Bronze Age aristocracies

An important hoard of bronzework found quite by chance at Corrymuckloch in Perthshire provides an insight into this Later Bronze Age

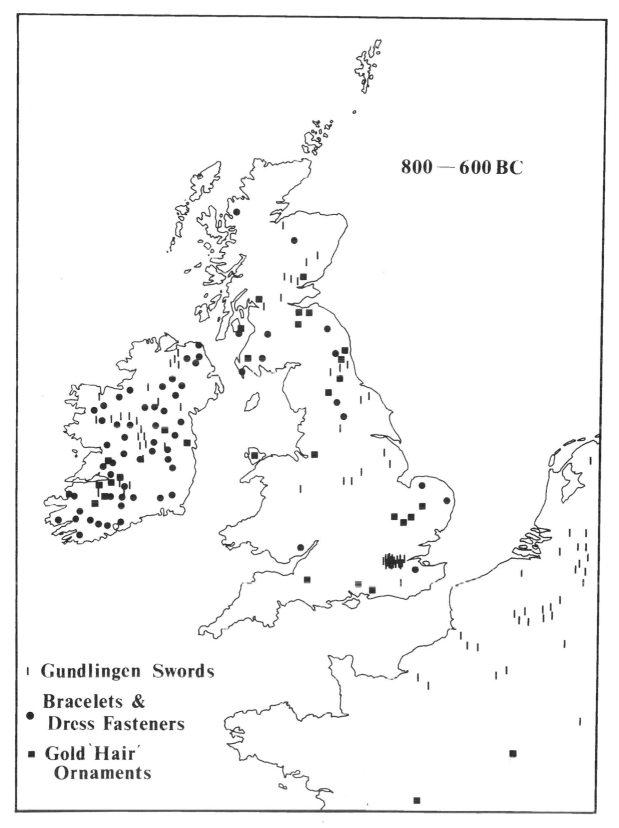

800 — 600 BC

| Gundlingen Swords

● Bracelets &
 Dress Fasteners

■ Gold 'Hair'
 Ornaments

world (8). In 1995, lying among the upcast from a drain through a peat bog, was found an array of fine bronzes: three socketed axes, a broken sword blade and a unique handled bowl or ladle, all dating to around 800 BC. Such hoards of metalwork, from bogs, rivers and other wet places, are characteristic of the Later Bronze Age in Scotland and indeed much of the rest of Britain and Ireland. Although richer than most, the Corrymuckloch find is not untypical. But who were the people who originally disposed of these objects and why did they do it?

Several features of the Corrymuckloch hoard hint at the status of its owners. To begin with, bronze was not easily available to all echelons of society. The procurement, transport and smelting of the necessary copper and tin ores all had to be organized before the actual process of manufacture could even begin. Elaborate objects like swords and fine vessels, requiring the time and energies of skilled craftsmen, would have been greatly prized. The owners of the Corrymuckloch hoard were clearly more than simple peasant farmers. They were part of an elite.

The Corrymuckloch ladle highlights another aspect of these Bronze Age elites. Ladles belong to a tradition of beaten bronze vessels, including buckets and cauldrons, associated with drinking and feasting. However, there is no vessel quite like that from Corrymuckloch anywhere else in the British Isles. In fact, to find parallels one has to go as far as northern Italy and Hungary. The Corrymuckloch sword too has overseas connections, being a variant of the 'Hallstatt' swords found widely across Later Bronze Age Europe. Clearly these objects were part of a Europe-wide cultural tradition where exotic and elaborate items associated with feasting, drinking and fighting were prized by local aristocratic families.

Whether in Greece, Italy, Central Europe or the British Isles, many Bronze Age societies seem to have shared certain very basic traits. Their culture was based on a 'heroic' view of society, where warrior aristocrats lorded over the lower orders, their power established and maintained

by the threat of violence and the conspicuous display of wealth. These male-dominated elites are manifested, for example, in rich burials throughout Central Europe and in the earliest representational art in the Mediterranean. Craftsmen and religious specialists occupied the next rung down the social order with the peasantry and unfree below that. Such generalizations can mask enormous differences, but it does seem likely that this broad structure, first established in Europe in the Bronze Age, was to underpin the subsequent and separate developments in many European societies over the next 1000 years and more, long after the complex web of Bronze Age social contacts had broken down.

The circumstances of the discovery of the Corrymuckloch hoard tell us even more about these cosmopolitan and aggressive elites. This cache of prized possessions had been placed in a bog, with no intention of recovery, the sword having first been deliberately broken. Almost all of the many hundreds of known Later Bronze Age objects have been found in similar circumstances; wealth destroyed and cast away in deliberate acts of sacrifice. Such gifts to the gods were at once a show of piety, an act of propitiation and a display of status and power.

Celtic languages

There is, by and large, a consensus that Celtic languages emerged in Europe during the Later Bronze Age and they were certainly dominant throughout the British Isles by the time of the Roman occupation. Indeed, the Greek writer Pytheas, writing as early as 325 BC and quoted by Diodorus Siculus in the first century BC, referred to Britain as the 'Pretanic Islands', and to Orkney as the 'Orcas', both clearly Celtic names. The Scottish tribal names and place-names recorded by the Greek geographer Ptolemy are mostly Celtic and the subsequent Early Historic kingdoms of the Picts, Scots and Britons all spoke Celtic languages. There is no such consensus, however, when it comes to the mechanisms by which Celtic languages evolved and spread.

8 The Corrymuckloch hoard from the Sma' Glen in Perthshire was discovered in 1995. Along with a deliberately snapped sword blade and three socketed axes, this group included a ladle or handled bowl, presently unique in Scotland. Across Europe, such vessels seem to have been associated with the aristocratic practices of feasting and drinking. The Corrymuckloch hoard, probably deposited around 800 BC, suggests that Scottish chiefs and their followers indulged with no less enthusiasm than their continental contemporaries.

The answer to this question once seemed fairly clear. Perhaps the most characteristic artefact of the Later Bronze Age in central and western Europe is the bronze slashing sword, like that in the Corrymuckloch hoard. Such swords, of European influence if not actual manufacture, are found along the major river systems of eastern Scotland (9). Surely then, this denotes a river-borne invasion of Celtic-speaking warriors, made almost invincible by their advanced military technology? This invasion hypothesis, however, is hard to sustain. As at Corrymuckloch, these swords were not casual losses from riverside skirmishes but were deposited as ritual offerings, following the same patterns of disposal as the dirks, rapiers and other bronzes of earlier centuries. Aside from the appearance of European-influenced metalwork, little else changed. Settlements, agriculture and ritual practices continued much as before, showing no signs of any disruptive population incursions.

In another sense, however, Celtic languages may well have come to Scotland with these swords. To understand the effects that the exchange networks of the Later Bronze Age would have had on language it is worth looking at the processes by which languages in general evolve and change.

It is easy to be too precious about language. As has often been said, a language is no more than a dialect with an army and a navy. Lacking the orthodoxy imposed by the nation state, Bronze Age Europe would have been a linguistically untidy continent with innumerable related languages and dialects. Many people would have been routinely bilingual or multilingual depending on their social mobility and status.

The distributions of prestige goods current in Scotland, Ireland and England from around 1200 BC show clear evidence of intensive and prolonged contacts (see 7). Each exchange, from the procurement of the ore to the handing over of the finished product to its final owner, involved a linguistic exchange, often between people whose first languages may have been mutually unintelligible. Such contacts represent one of the main mechanisms by which languages change and spread. Exchange requires a lingua franca, often in the form of a pidgin version of one dominant language, eventually mixing with native languages to produce creoles; effectively new languages.

It was the existence of East African trade networks during the present millennium that enabled the spread of the trade variety of Swahili, eventually spoken by upwards of 30 million people. Similarly, in Indonesia, speakers of Malay encompass hundreds of diverse groups united through maritime trading networks. Neither of these language spreads came about through invasion or colonization. John Waddell and Jane Conroy have suggested that a proto-Celtic language could have acted as one of many trade languages in the Later Bronze Age, spoken by those groups in western Europe involved in long-distance exchange. As such it might have formed creoles with indigenous languages, some of which may already have been closely related. Once formed, creoles can themselves hybridize with other languages. The wholesale movement of population is only one, and perhaps not a particularly common, mode of language replacement.

As well as social and economic convenience, language spread can be precipitated by purely symbolic factors. The use of Latin in Christian liturgical practice is an obvious example. Slang, accent and inflection are used, even today, to denote group affiliation and to exclude outsiders, while the speech patterns of the social elite are emulated by other social groups keen to 'talk properly'. Such phenomena are quite familiar to us today, but in societies where standard speech was not enshrined in written documents or promoted by mass media, they would have created much more fluid and localized variations in speech than we are used to.

9 European-influenced slashing swords were at the forefront of Later Bronze Age technology and are found, mainly in ritual deposits, along the eastern river valleys.

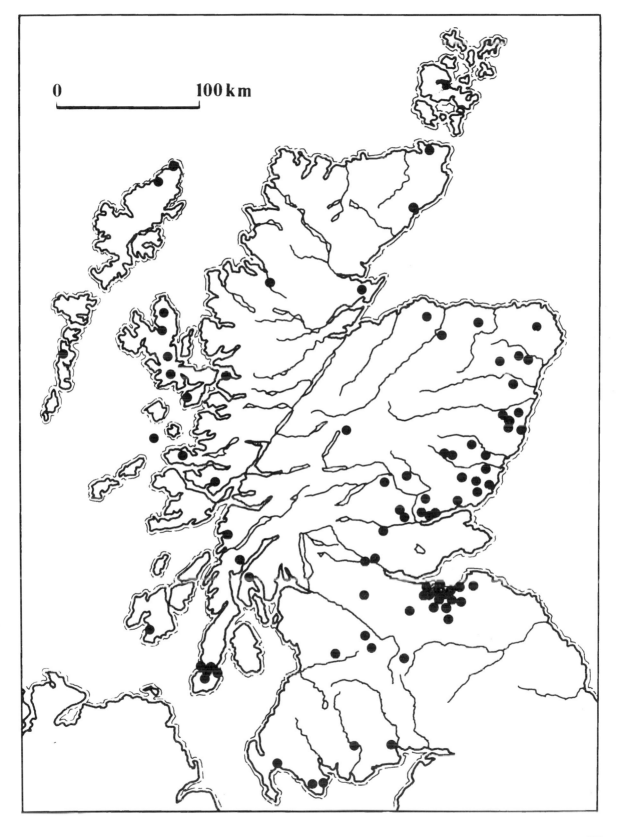

0   100 km

From what we know of Later Bronze Age elites it is more than likely that they would have adopted modes of speech that distinguished them from the lower orders, in much the same way as they adopted exotic weapons and ornaments. Waddell and Conroy have pointed out that more recent elites, like the ill-fated Russian aristocracy with their predilection for speaking French, have done exactly the same.

The spread of Celtic languages across the British Isles was undoubtedly a complex business, probably taking place over many centuries and spurred by the same processes that led to the arrival of European-influenced swords and jewellery. It almost certainly involved a degree of language-mixing among the more mobile elements of society, traders, elite families and war-bands, and the development of linguistic differences between social classes. There would have been periods when dialects grew together and other times when they grew apart. There were probably also episodes when larger communities moved, perhaps pushed by famine, disease or social instability. In a linguistic sense, then, it is most unlikely that there was ever a single, identifiable 'coming of the Celts'.

A Celtic inheritance?

It would be easy to exaggerate the importance of the Bronze Age 'European Union'. Throughout the continent, many communities would have comprised only isolated farmers, and the great majority of people would probably never have travelled more than a few kilometres from their place of birth. Nonetheless, there were clearly intensive contacts between those in positions of power within society and we should not underestimate the degree to which these elite groups influenced and were emulated by the rest of the population.

By around 700 BC, however, the Europe-wide networks of exchange were beginning to break down. One reason, though probably not the only one, was the collapse of the bronze industry as iron became more widely used for the manufacture of tools and weapons. Iron ore was much more widely available than copper or tin, so there was little need to maintain long-distance contacts. In some upland areas of Britain the cumulative effects of climatic deterioration over several centuries, the exhaustion of soils and the spread of peat may have exacerbated, if not caused, social and economic collapse. Regional elites may have become increasingly unable to engage in long-distance exchange as their local resource base slumped.

After 700 BC communities in Scotland seem to have become rather more inward-looking and self-contained and we start to see the marked regionalization of material culture. As we will note in the next two chapters, enormous effort was expended on building monumental houses and forts, while extravagant offerings to the gods seem to have declined or even disappeared for several centuries. Yet the Bronze Age webs of exchange had lasting effects. People throughout the British Isles and beyond now had an unprecedented communality of language and culture, so that, despite the ensuing centuries of fragmentation and insularity, there would be certain similarities in the ways in which they evolved and adapted. These similarities were such that when these communities next came into closer contact, during the expansion of the Roman empire, they were, at least superficially, sufficiently similar to be regarded by outsiders as a coherent cultural group.

This 'Celticization' of Scotland had been complex and protracted, involving Europe-wide developments in language and social change. Yet, although the mobility of individuals and small, influential groups was crucial, there was no single invasion, nor indeed was there any identifiable 'homeland'. The ancestral land of the Scottish Celts was Scotland itself.

3

House and home

While there are sporadic examples of substantial, even monumental, houses in earlier periods, such as in the Neolithic village of Skara Brae in Orkney, the greatest building projects of the first farming communities were religious monuments and tombs. From the Bronze Age, however, the focus switched to houses.

Bronze and Iron Age houses are all around us. Scattered across the uplands of Scotland, particularly in the north and east, are the remains of hut circles; the worn-down walls of once-imposing prehistoric roundhouses. In the lowlands the last traces of similar timber buildings, flattened by innumerable centuries of ploughing, show up as distinctive circular marks in ripening crops. Our lochs are dotted with the scoured remnants of artificial islet dwellings known as crannogs, while, in the far north and west, broch towers like Mousa in Shetland and Dun Carloway in Lewis dominate the landscape even today (see **colour plate 2**).

Although some of these architectural traditions are uniquely Scottish, substantial houses of one sort or another are found throughout Britain, from Wessex to Orkney. While their ancestry can be traced back into the Bronze Age, they flourished in the middle centuries of the first millennium BC, after the collapse of the bronze industry and its associated networks of exchange, and following the demise of the sword-wielding aristocracies whose needs it served. Ring-ditch houses, crannogs and Atlantic roundhouses seem to reflect the more fragmented social conditions that followed, when local communities with a good deal of independence could flaunt their status by the building of fine and elaborate houses.

Iron Age people

Before looking at the range of Iron Age houses it is useful to consider the people who built and inhabited them. The general lack of burial evidence for most of the first millennium BC makes it hard to reconstruct even the basic characteristics of Iron Age communities, such as life expectancy, infant mortality, age and gender structure. In the absence of such information, however, it is worth making a few general points about pre-industrial populations based on what is currently the best-studied prehistoric community in Scotland: those buried in the Neolithic tomb at Isbister in Orkney. The bodies from Isbister represent a cross-section of age and sex groups, leading the excavator to conclude that most members of the community, aside from very young infants, ended up in the monument.

Average heights of 170cm (5ft 7in) for men and 163cm (5ft 4in) for women in the Isbister tomb were close to modern averages, the differences probably resulting from a relatively poor diet. All were highly muscular, by modern standards, but many showed in their bones the effects of harsh working conditions from early childhood. Several of the women had skull deformities caused by carrying loads by means of a 'brow-band', and more than half the adults exhibited some degenerative disease of the spine resulting from heavy labour.

Perhaps the most striking features of the Isbister population were their low life expectancy and high levels of child mortality. Most of those surviving to puberty died before reaching 30 and only a few individuals could hope to reach 50 (most of the latter being men, the rigours of childbirth evidently adding to the stresses on the female population). This would have had profound effects on the ways in which communities were structured: the population would have been young, with children probably working in the fields and tending the flocks and herds at an early age. Since old age was a relatively rare achievement, it is probable that the elderly commanded respect and perhaps held a venerated status. The composition of individual households would inevitably have been quite varied and probably based on extended rather than nuclear families, due to the unpredictable loss of individuals of all ages through disease and injury.

Yet these people were by no means uniquely unfortunate. Many characteristics of the Isbister population are all but inescapable in pre-industrial farming communities and similar studies of medieval and later burials on the Hebridean island of Ensay revealed strikingly similar rates of child mortality in much more recent times.

There are problems, however, in making direct comparisons between the dead of Isbister and the peoples of Iron Age Scotland around 2000 years later. To begin with we must remember that the people of Isbister were as remote in time from the Iron Age population as the latter are from us. Perhaps more importantly, there is evidence throughout the first millennium BC of marked social differentiation of a kind not seen among their rather egalitarian Neolithic ancestors. The privileged classes may well have laboured less and thus avoided many of the ills suffered by the early tomb-builders. Similarly, those in the relatively lush farmlands of the south and east may have led rather easier lives than their upland neighbours. We know nothing

as yet of prehistoric medicine and thus can have no knowledge of potentially significant differences in the treatment of disease and injury between the two periods. Doubtless both communities had their healers and their own traditional bodies of medicinal practice.

Cultural factors too will have determined the nature and organization of prehistoric households. In many non-western societies, settlement compounds and houses are divided up according to age, rank and gender; with certain areas restricted to men or women, or perhaps to the head of the household. We cannot tell whether societies in the first millennium practised monogamy or polygamy, another factor which would have had radical implications for the composition of the household and the organization of domestic life. Nonetheless, the Neolithic people of Isbister give at least some clues as to what we might expect of prehistoric rural populations in Scotland, and we can reasonably expect that Iron Age households would have had a composition quite unlike those of today.

Bronze Age houses in the Sutherland glens

The most common prehistoric houses visible in the landscape today are hut circles. This rather antiquated term encompasses a wide variety of architectural forms that need share little more than a tendency to decay into a ring-shaped earthen bank. Many were originally imposing and elaborate buildings to which the rather disparaging term 'hut' does little justice. These roundhouses are among the most common prehistoric remains in the Scottish landscape, with more than 2000 known in Sutherland alone. They often occur in loose agglomerations straggling across extensive areas of moorland, where they have escaped the ravages of later ploughing, surrounded by the remains of irregular field plots and clearance cairns (10).

Some of the earliest hut circles yet known were excavated recently at Achany Glen, near Lairg in Sutherland. Between about 2000 and 1500 BC this glen, like many in Sutherland, was home to numerous families living in large timber probably served as sleeping or working areas. This sort of radial division was to be a recurrent feature throughout the Iron Age, appearing in its clearest form almost 2000 years later in the wheelhouses of the Western Isles and Shetland (see below).

Hut circles dating to the Later Bronze Age have been excavated at Kilphedir in Sutherland. One of these (hut circle I) had a floor area of around 11 by 10m (36 by 33ft); significantly larger than some of the rather later broch towers (**11**). A ring of internal posts probably held an upper floor as well as supporting the roof, the rafters of which rested on walls of stone and earth. This building was occupied long enough to require major remodelling of its internal posts on at least two

10 A covering of snow helps to show up the full extent of this sprawling prehistoric landscape at Pitcarmick in Perthshire, some 350m (1150ft) above sea level. Most of the small mounds are clearance cairns, formed by early farmers as they cleared the land of stones. Two large hut circles can be seen at the centre top of the photograph.

roundhouses and farming the surrounding land. Construction methods varied from house to house: some were of 'wigwam' design, with the rafters of the conical roof supported directly on the ground; some had circular walls founded on a bank of earth and faced with wattle panels; while others had roofs supported on internal rings of posts. The designs probably evolved gradually over time, but we have too few dated examples for this early period to detect such changes.

Inside these houses the available space was divided by means of timber partitions set around the periphery, while the central floors were left open to form the communal focus of the house for cooking and eating. The peripheral bays seem to have been floored with timber planks and

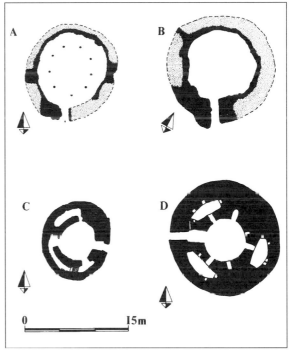

11 A comparison of the ground-plans of hut circles I and V (A and B) at Kilphedir in Sutherland, the complex roundhouse of Dun Bharabhat in Lewis (C), and the broch tower of Mousa in Shetland (D), shows that hut circles could contain as much, if not more, space than the more lauded brochs. Given that many may have had upper floors, and bearing in mind that they tend to occur in groups, hut circle settlements may often have been rather more substantial than many of those represented by brochs.

occasions. As before, domestic life was centred on the large hearth towards the middle of the building while the periphery may have been partitioned off, as at Lairg. When occupied, this substantial house, one of two almost identical structures at Kilphedir, was probably at least as impressive as many later brochs (**12**).

During the first millennium BC the Sutherland hut circles seem to have become rather more complex in design, although their overall numbers may have reduced, and instead of clustered villages we tend to find isolated farmsteads. There was a tendency for the walls of these later buildings to incorporate more stone and for doorways to be lengthened to create more formal entrance passages. Some even had cells and galleries within their walls, mirroring

12 Hut circle I at Kilphedir probably dates to the Later Bronze Age (judging from the 'flat-rimmed' pottery found within it) and was a long-lived and imposing building to which the rather pejorative description 'hut circle' seems ill-suited. Reconstructions, such as this cutaway view, are based on a combination of building experiment and deduction from the excavated evidence. The internal post-ring, which was replaced at least twice during the lifetime of the building, probably carried an upper floor as well as helping support the roof. Like most roundhouses, the building would have had a conical thatched roof with a pitch approximating to 45° to aid the run-off of rainwater.

the development of broch architecture, as Horace Fairhurst, one of the excavators of Kilphedir, observed. The last of the Kilphedir houses (hut circle V), occupied in the later centuries BC, typifies these changes with its stone-faced wall at least 1.5m (5ft) high, an intra-mural gallery, and an entrance passage around 4.5m (15ft) long.

Variations on a theme: timber roundhouses in the south and east

Platform settlements

Just as the excavations at Lairg have pushed the dates of hut circles firmly back into the Bronze Age, recent work in Upper Clydesdale has shown an equally precocious development of timber roundhouses in the south. At the site of Lintshie Gutter, more than thirty platforms cut into the hillside mark the stances for roundhouses formed of earthen walls faced with wattle and daub. Inside were the hearths, cooking pits, pottery and querns used by the inhabitants. Charcoal from the buildings has been dated well before 1500 BC and the settlement was clearly occupied over many centuries. Similar settlements, such as at Green Knowe in Peeblesshire, may have persisted as late as 800 BC.

These 'platform' settlements are common throughout the southern uplands and we must assume that the houses they once supported were equally common in lowland areas where platforms were not required. These sites are hard to find but one at Myrehead, near Falkirk, revealed three timber roundhouses dating to before 750 BC, with dimensions and internal features similar to those of the platform houses at Green Knowe.

House platforms are also found in some early hilltop enclosures, as at Eildon Hill North in Roxburghshire (see chapter 4). However, the structures that occupied these platforms probably varied widely in design and construction over time and from place to place.

Ring-ditch and ring-groove houses

Some early roundhouses can be detected without the giveaway platforms. These are known as ring-groove and ring-ditch houses because of the distinctive marks they leave in unploughed upland pastures, like those of the Cheviot Hills. Ring-groove houses were built of timber, their conical thatched roofs resting on an inner ring of stout posts and an outer wall of close-spaced timbers. This outer wall was set in a circular foundation trench and it is this that can sometimes be identified as a low groove in the ground surface. Sometimes two concentric grooves are discernible and these double ring-groove houses have been identified as a particularly early variant.

Survey of the Bowmont Valley in the Cheviots has shown that some settlements enclosed by timber palisades contained six or more of these double ring-groove houses aligned along a central 'street'. They are also sometimes found within early hilltop settlements like Burnswark Hill, Annandale and White Meldon in Peeblesshire (see chapter 4) but seem to have largely fallen out of use by around 500 BC. In the Bowmont Valley their remains are sometimes overlain by ring-ditch houses; a related but probably slightly later form, perhaps dating from around 700–300 BC, and it is these ring-ditch houses that occupy many of the southern hillforts discussed in chapter 4.

Although not uncommon in the southern uplands, it is in the arable lowlands of south and east Scotland that ring-ditch houses have been studied most intensively (13). This has been mostly due to a burst of archaeological activity in the late 1970s and early 1980s when rescue excavations were carried out on a fort at Broxmouth, East Lothian, an unenclosed village at Douglasmuir in Angus, and other sites threatened mostly by quarrying.

Ring-ditch houses in general conform to a remarkably consistent ground-plan, presumably reflecting a widespread and fairly coherent architectural tradition. The space inside was organized into concentric zones. In the centre was a level or slightly domed circular area, often curiously devoid of the trappings of domestic life, like hearths and cooking pits. However, the presence of two hearths in a recently excavated example, high on Culhawk Hill in Angus, suggests that similar fittings on lowland sites may have been obliterated by centuries of ploughing.

Surrounding this central zone was a ditch, often paved and usually quite shallow (although

13 Aerial photography can often give us a glimpse of prehistoric sites in the lowlands where all surface traces have long since been removed by the plough. The ditches, post holes and pits of ancient settlements, like this pair of ring-ditch houses at Hawkhill Quarry in Angus, fill up with soil that is often deeper or different in texture to that of the surrounding field. In suitable conditions, especially in dry summers, this can affect the growth of crops and produce colour patterns that reflect the layout of the original settlement.

ring of posts probably supported an upper timber floor.

One theory to explain the peculiar architecture of the ring-ditch house suggests that cattle could have been stalled and overwintered in the paved 'ditch'. The animals would thus have been protected from the worst of the winter weather, at the same time providing warmth for the human occupants and a readily collectable source of dung to fertilize the surrounding fields. A typical ring-ditch house could probably have accommodated up to thirty cattle. The human inhabitants, meanwhile, would have lived on the timber first floor, hence the general absence of ground-level domestic fittings (14). The central part of the ground floor would have served principally as a storage area for animal feed and other agricultural products. Its storage capacity of around fifty tonnes of hay would have been quite capable of supporting thirty cattle through the winter months.

This concept of a prehistoric 'byre-house' has more modern parallels. The well-known blackhouses of the Hebrides, for example, were home to cattle as well as people until quite recently. It has also been suggested that where several ring-ditches occur on a single site, some may have been exclusively barns while others were exclusively houses. Nonetheless, the interpretation has its problems, not least of which is the rather daunting prospect of providing enough water for the cattle on sites not always conveniently situated near a source of fresh water.

It has been calculated that upwards of 650 trees, each yielding over 6m (20ft) of timber,

the ditches at Douglasmuir in Angus were up to 2m (6ft) deep. At Broxmouth fort in East Lothian, where the most detailed evidence was recovered, the roofs were supported on inner rings of posts and an outer plank wall, either side of the ditch, while a rather slighter middle

14 This cutaway drawing shows an artist's impression of daily life as it might have been in a ring-ditch house around 500 BC. Like many of the larger hut circles, these were elaborate and spacious buildings, and it has been suggested that they may have been used to over-winter cattle as well as for human habitation. Some of the ring-ditch houses inside the fort at Broxmouth in East Lothian were remodelled and rebuilt up to five times on the same site, probably over several centuries.

would have been swallowed up in the construction of a single ring-ditch house. Judging from the considerable energy expended on their construction it is not too fanciful to imagine that their interiors may have been finished and maintained with equal care; their wattle-and-daub walls may have been brightly painted or hung with decorated hides and textile adornments, while wooden furniture may have stood upon on their timber floors.

Whatever the details of their construction, we can be confident that ring-ditch houses were big, ostentatious buildings by the standards of what had gone before, their façades often embellished by airy porches and massive timber swing-doors. That these buildings were as much about prestige and status as about the practicalities of warmth and shelter is demonstrated by the recently excavated example on Culhawk Hill in Angus. This building sits at more than 300m (984ft) above sea level, overlooking the fertile expanses of Strathmore; it is inconceivable that anyone would build a house some 20m (66ft) in diameter and around 10m (33ft) high in such an absurdly exposed hilltop location unless their aim was to dominate the landscape and the valley below.

Crannogs
In some parts of Scotland, particularly the Highlands and the south-west, timber

33

roundhouses were commonly built on artificial islets of timber or stone, known as crannogs (from the Gaelic root word 'crann' meaning wood). Crannogs were generally constructed on foundations of stone, timber or brushwood, sometimes utilizing natural outcrops. They were usually sited close to the shores of inland lochs from which they were reached by stone causeways, wooden gangways, or by log boats, of which examples up to 13m (43ft) long have been found preserved in the loch mud (15).

Aside from a solitary example in South Wales, crannogs are found only in Ireland and Scotland, where they are recorded as late as the eighteenth century (some even serving as refuges in the aftermath of the '45 Rising). However, their origins lie much earlier. The oldest site that can be meaningfully called a crannog is Eilean Domhnuill on North Uist, a largely if not wholly artificial islet dating to the Neolithic period, around 3000 BC. Most, however, seem to date to the period from the

15 This artist's impression of an Iron Age crannog is based on the excavated example in Milton Loch in Kirkcudbrightshire, which has been radiocarbon dated to around 700–300 BC.

Later Bronze Age to the Early Historic period, with re-occupation thereafter.

Many crannogs were discovered and excavated towards the end of the nineteenth century, when hundreds of lochs were drained to improve land for agriculture. The waterlogged conditions on these sites meant that many perishable, organic materials that would long since have decayed on dry-land sites survived virtually intact. Wooden bowls, barrels and churns, pins, pegs and mallets and even a shoe-last were recovered from Buiston crannog in Ayrshire. Other sites produced well-preserved rope, ladles and scoops and boxes, filling out the meagre record of stone, metal and pottery objects that survive from contemporary dry-land sites, and showing something of what has been lost elsewhere.

More recently crannogs have been studied by underwater archaeologists, using modern excavation techniques. Excavations at Oakbank in Loch Tay, for example, have recovered such casual debris as grains, seeds, nuts, animal droppings and insects, all of which help reconstruct the Iron Age environment of the site and the life-style of its occupants. This work has shown that Oakbank was home to a small community of Iron Age farmers herding animals, growing crops and gathering wild plant foods on the fertile lochside (**16**).

Nobody yet, however, has answered fully the basic question of why such immense efforts were expended to construct these great island platforms, a precarious enterprise demanding substantial resources of skill, time and timber, before work even started on the house itself. Defence may be one answer; crannogs would presumably have been defended relatively easily against a small band of raiders attempting either to cross the causeway or to land a boat, though they would remain vulnerable to attacks by fire or siege. Crannogs would also have served to protect stock from predators, such as wolves and bears, that would have roamed the Iron Age glens. However, a stout palisade would probably have provided equal protection for considerably less effort and expense.

As with ring-ditch houses it appears that, whatever their practical defensive capability, fashion and prestige played a major role in the construction of crannogs. As elsewhere, the land-holding farmers of the Highland glens and the south-west had sufficient resources at their disposal to display their wealth and status to their neighbours, and to stamp on the very landscape their legitimate tenancy of the locale.

16 This map shows the locations of crannogs in Loch Tay and of homesteads in Glen Lyon to the north. It seems likely that both groups represent broadly contemporary farms situated for convenient access to the limited patches of good land along the two valleys; the crannogs exploit the shallow margins of the loch, while the homesteads, with no natural defences, rely on thicker walls and stone construction.

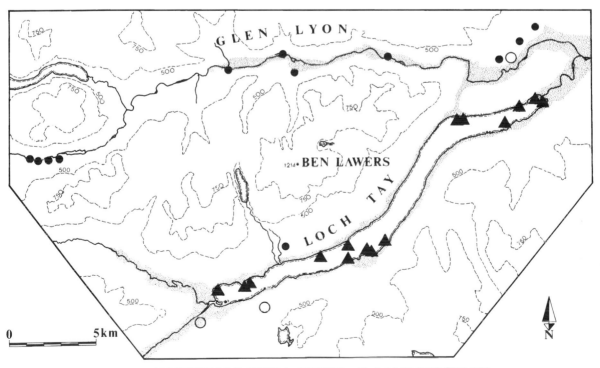

▲ CRANNOGS ● HOMESTEADS ○ HILL FORTS   LAND BELOW 150 m

Towers in the north

While reconstruction drawings can give some sense of how impressive the timber roundhouses might once have been, it is perhaps only with the broch towers of the north and west that we can gain a real sense of the visual impact of such buildings and of the central role of the roundhouse in Iron Age life. Yet brochs and duns have tended to be studied in isolation, long regarded as defensive retreats from the petty warfare and piracy thought to have plagued regions remote from the mainstream of the Celtic world. It is only in recent years that they have become widely recognized as houses, albeit stoutly built and defensible ones, rather than simply as occasional refuges.

Broch towers

In their final form, broch towers represent masterpieces of roundhouse architecture. Mousa in Shetland, the archetypal broch tower, still stands 13.3m (43ft) tall, its grim, grey outer shell punctured only by a single door, its scale and intricacy far exceeding any more recent dry-stone structure (**17**).

Despite regional variations, broch-building involved certain well-established principles, best illustrated at Dun Carloway in Lewis where the broch structure has been neatly exposed by its partial collapse (see **colour plate 2**). Like all broch towers, Dun Carloway was formed of two concentric dry-stone walls, bonded by rows of slabs. These slabs formed a series of superimposed galleries linked by stairs within the walls, while openings in the inner wall gave access to upper timber floors that have long since disappeared (**18**).

Other architectural elaborations augment this basic design. Ledges, or 'scarcements', projecting from the inner wall, for example, would have supported timber floors and rafters. Perhaps most intriguingly, vertical rows of small openings known as 'voids' ascend the interiors of many broch towers. In the case of Mousa there are four such rows, the function of which has never been adequately explained. One common theory is that they served to ease the weight of stone above the entrances to cells and galleries, yet this seems an unlikely justification for the creation of what were

17 The broch tower of Mousa in Shetland is one of the best preserved prehistoric buildings in Britain, standing close to its original height at around 13m (43ft) tall.

18 The partial collapse of the broch tower of Dun Telve in Glenelg has exposed the galleries that run between its walls.

potentially dangerous weak points in the structure of the building.

John Hope, an architect with an interest in prehistoric buildings, has recently suggested an explanation of the way in which these various distinctive features might have combined to produce a functioning building. In his model, the galleries would have prevented wind-driven rain and snow from percolating through the inner wall. In winter, the rows of voids would have let the warm air from the hearth circulate in the galleries, keeping them dry and warm, and protecting the living space inside the tower from the extremes of weather. In summer, the same principle would have spread heat from the sun around the building.

John Hope's model neatly solves some of the long-standing puzzles of broch design. For example, all broch towers were provided with galleries and stairs. Yet only at Mousa is there proper access all the way to the wall-head. At Dun Carloway, for example, the upper galleries are far too narrow for an adult to pass through,

and were certainly not intended to give access to the roof. But in Hope's reconstruction their primary purpose was simply to let air circulate, even though some of the lower, wider galleries were probably also used to allow passage between floors.

Another important observation made by John Hope is that the inner walls at ground floor level tend to be rather less well finished than those above. At some sites, like Dun Carloway, the ground floor is markedly uneven, with large outcrops of rock projecting in places. This suggests that the main living space may have been sited at first-floor level while the ground floor was used to overwinter animals and store agricultural produce, much as has been suggested for ring-ditch houses in the south (19). Indeed, this might explain why the walls of many broch towers are solid-based, with the galleries beginning only at first-floor level, since this is the level at which the hearth would have burned.

Early Atlantic roundhouses

With their wealth of architectural detail, it is easy to see why the well-preserved broch towers

19 A cutaway drawing showing life in the broch tower of Dun Carloway in Lewis. The ground floor is used for animal shelter and for storage, while domestic activity is concentrated on the upper floors.

have captured the imagination of archaeologists and laymen for so long. Spectacular broch towers like Mousa and Dun Carloway, however, represent the culmination of centuries of development of the Atlantic roundhouse tradition, which had its origins in rather humbler buildings: houses that were essentially stone translations of the southern roundhouse form.

Strangely, in Orkney and Shetland, later to become the broch heartlands, there seems to have been no real tradition of Bronze Age hut circle construction. Instead there was a continuation of much older, cellular building styles with their roots in the Neolithic (**20**). Small oval cellular buildings found widely across Shetland, for example, perpetuated structural forms found more than 1000 years earlier at sites like Stanydale and Scord of Brouster, and in Orkney at Skara Brae. But this apparent conservatism was to change radically from around 700 BC with the appearance of the first roundhouses.

The first identifiable ancestors of the broch towers were a series of thick-walled dry-stone roundhouses that appeared in Orkney sometime around 600 BC. Like the crannogs further south, these were mostly isolated farmsteads, the best known being that at Bu, excavated in the late 1970s. Although their walls were massively thick (some were even periodically enlarged by adding extra skins of masonry), they seem to have lacked the distinctive features, such as galleries, cells and stairs, associated with later broch towers.

The Bu roundhouse floor was divided by tall flagstones into a series of separate rooms. However, rather than the simple radial plan found in roundhouses further south, the maze of interconnecting rooms seems to reflect the cellular interiors of older buildings in Orkney and Shetland, only now squeezed inside a circular shell of masonry. Despite outward appearances, then, the patterns and routines of daily life probably carried on much as before.

Yet why adopt the roundhouse form at all if it was simply to be used to cloak a rather traditional cellular interior? After all, roundhouses have significant disadvantages in the wind-chilled northern climate. For example, while the cells of older buildings could be easily roofed with stone slabs or stumps of driftwood, the new roundhouses demanded altogether more substantial timbers, not to mention rather more advanced carpentry skills. The new buildings were also substantially taller (the walls of the

20 In the Later Bronze Age and Early Iron Age many communities in upland areas of Scotland used a distinctive cooking method in which meat was boiled in a water trough kept on the boil by plunging in heated stones. The heaps of fire-cracked stones that accumulated around these cooking places are known as burnt mounds. At Liddle in Orkney, excavation of the mound revealed the remains of a contemporary cellular house.

early roundhouse at St Boniface in Orkney standing at least 3m (10ft) high), and thus, unlike the rather more squat buildings of earlier times, exposed to the full blast of the Orcadian winds.

It is difficult to escape the conclusion that this wilful disregard for scarce timber, ease of construction and environmental suitability was completely intentional and that even the earliest Atlantic roundhouses represent ostentatious symbols of wealth and status.

Towards towers

Over the ensuing centuries we can begin to detect the gradual elaboration of these Atlantic roundhouses and their adoption over much of the Highlands and Islands. While probably never attaining the grandeur of the later towers, new, 'complex' roundhouses began to incorporate novel architectural features. The design of the roundhouse at Crosskirk in Caithness, for example, smacks of innovation and experiment. This structure, probably built before 400 BC, has cells and a staircase built into its wall, even though the instability of its clay core would have prevented any tower-like superstructure.

Like the roundhouse form itself, galleries can be viewed as a regional reflection of a wider phenomenon. Galleries also appear, for example, in the broadly contemporary developed hut circles of Sutherland, while the paved ditches in southern ring-ditch houses may well have served a similar function and, like broch galleries, seem to have marked off areas around the periphery of the roundhouse for some specialized use. Souterrains, curving subterranean cellars found in settlements in many parts of Scotland, may be yet another manifestation of this architectural trend (see chapter 5).

The emergence of broch towers from this background of architectural development is best seen at Howe of Howe in Orkney, the only such site yet to have been subject to near-total excavation. The first roundhouse at Howe was built around 400 BC, although even that overlay an earlier village and an already ancient Neolithic chambered tomb. This structure

occupied a small enclosure and had walls at least 4m (13ft) thick. Other details, however, are hard to reconstruct, because some time before 200 BC the house was largely dismantled and incorporated within the fabric of a new, complex roundhouse.

The second roundhouse was an imposing structure with walls 3.5m (11ft) thick. It may even have been a broch tower although it did not survive high enough for us to be sure. Within the walls two staircases led to upper timber floors, while the entrance passage gave access to two small cells. Yet impressive as it no doubt was, this second roundhouse was superseded, between 200 BC and AD 100, by the next and grandest phase in the settlement's history: the building of a full-blown broch tower with, clustered around its base, a planned village of subsidiary houses.

Broch villages

There were probably at least twenty broch villages in Orkney alone, and still more in Caithness (21). Probably the most impressive of all is at Gurness in Orkney where the symmetry and order of the settlement exceeds even that at Howe. But the village at Howe remains the only one to have been extensively excavated in modern times, and the only one where the time depth of the settlement can yet be fully appreciated.

The 5.5m (18ft) thick walls of the broch tower at Howe suggest that the centrepiece of the village was an exceptionally tall and imposing structure, enveloping the foundations of the earlier roundhouses. Around it was laid out a series of cellular stone buildings, each with its own yard, filling virtually all the remaining space within the enclosure. Standard fittings, such as cupboards and ovens, within each of these buildings served to reinforce the integrity of the village's design.

Broch villages were powerful statements of social control. Whereas before, numerous land-holding families had each expressed their own local independence and status through the early roundhouses, the very architecture of broch

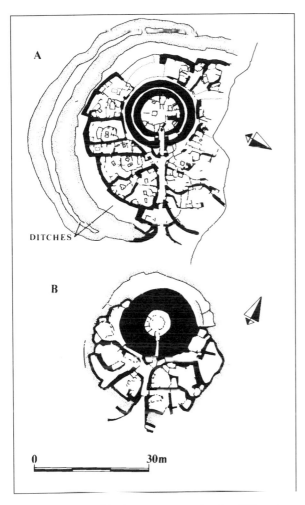

21 Broch villages like those at Gurness (top) and Howe in Orkney seem to represent the architectural embodiment of social control. The cellular homes of lower ranking families huddle in the shadow of the central tower which dominates the community, just as the earlier roundhouses dominated the farming landscape.

villages now graded the inhabitants according to rank, with the head family firmly ensconced at the centre of village life. It is easy to imagine how a child growing up in the cellular sprawl of the Gurness or Howe villages inevitably would have come to regard the authority of the broch-dwellers as a fixed and unchangeable part of the natural order of things. The tower would have been central to daily life, its constant maintenance, repair and re-roofing periodically reinforcing social roles and obligations among the villagers

Gradually, it seems, society in the north and west had become more centralized and certain people, like the head families at Howe and Gurness, had become dominant over their peers. Their already rather grand houses were rebuilt as elaborate towers with the homes of dependent families gathered around the base of their walls. In chapter 8 we will see just how powerful some of these tower-dwelling families may have been.

Wheelhouses

However, broch villages did not emerge everywhere. In Shetland and the Western Isles, despite the isolated grandeur of towers like Mousa and Dun Carloway, broch villages seem to have been entirely absent. Instead, by around the last century BC, when the Orcadian broch villages were occupied, many of the less elaborate Atlantic roundhouses had fallen into ruin. In some areas they appear to have been usurped as the standard settlement form of the day by an entirely novel type of building: the wheelhouse.

Wheelhouses are so called because of their distinctive ground plan in which a series of regularly spaced stone piers radiates from the centre like the spokes of a wheel (22). These buildings are extremely common in the Western Isles and are also found in Shetland, where a particularly fine series of wheelhouses was built around the abandoned 'complex' roundhouse at Jarlshof. Remarkably, however, despite more than a century of intensive archaeological exploration, none are yet known in Orkney. Indeed it seems that the areas where broch villages are found and those where wheelhouses occur may have been mutually exclusive.

The recent excavation of a well-preserved wheelhouse settlement at Cnip in Lewis has shown something of the architectural skill of the wheelhouse builders (23). The main wheelhouse at Cnip was built by first lining the sides of a great pit in the coastal sand dunes with a single skin of walling. Next the narrow stone pillars or piers (the spokes of the wheel) were set in place,

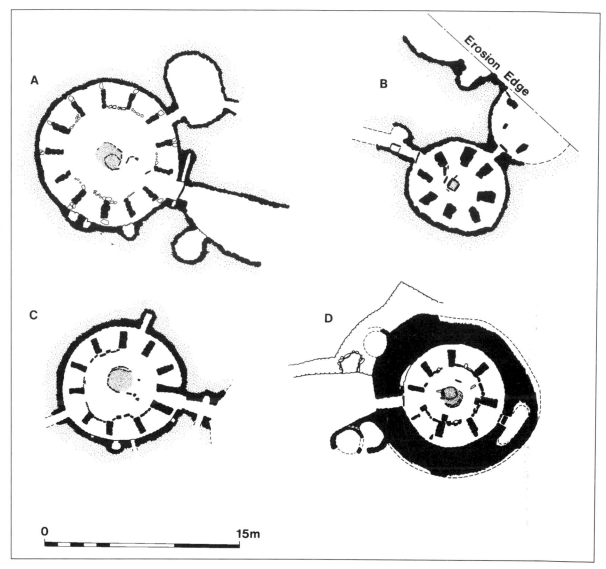

22 Wheelhouses derive their name from their distinctive shape. These plans are from various excavated examples in the Western Isles: a. Sollas, North Uist, b. Cnip, Lewis, c. Kilpheder, South Uist, d. Clettraval, North Uist.

rising from a single stone's thickness to support corbelled stone roofs over each of the cells. This was an intricate operation involving enormous skill in dry-stone building. Yet it was not approached in a wholly pragmatic way. During the building process numerous offerings, such as pottery vessels, animal skulls and joints of meat, were carefully placed within the fabric of the walls and below the floors (see chapter 7).

Once the stone-built parts of the building were complete, a timber roof was erected over the central area. Even in a small wheelhouse like that at Cnip, this roof rose to around 6m (20ft) above the hearth that burned in the middle of the house. While from the outside little more than a simple conical roof would have been visible, poking above the sand dune surface, this would have concealed a refined and accomplished architectural design.

Yet, unlike broch towers, wheelhouses were eminently practical as well as monumental buildings. The short span of the central area meant that no long timbers were needed for the roof. Because they were usually dug into sand-hills or the ruins of older buildings, most wheelhouses were sheltered, warm and well insulated.

While broch towers were outwardly monumental, an unwelcoming edifice of featureless masonry, wheelhouses were designed to be impressive on the inside. It is easy to imagine how imposing the elegant piers and high roof would have appeared to a visitor emerging from the long narrow entrance passage into the hearth-lit interior. Indeed, the nature of wheelhouse architecture suggests that people were now welcomed in each other's homes and implies rather more social integration than had been evident for many centuries.

This openness, along with the social order inherent in contemporary broch villages, perhaps reflects the emergence of more stable and cohesive societies throughout the north and west by the first century BC. Farmers in the islands clearly had some confidence that their homes were unlikely to be attacked, or their lands taken by force. It is hard to see how land rights and the social order could be guaranteed without the existence of some overriding authority, presumably vested in a social elite. It is even possible, as we shall see in chapter 8, that political power over all of these island groups rested with a handful of individuals: perhaps Orcadian chiefs or kings resident in broch villages like Gurness.

The end of the roundhouse

By the second century AD most wheelhouses seem to have either fallen into decay or been remodelled as cellular buildings reminiscent of those of earlier centuries. Similar cellular buildings also came to dominate the Orcadian broch villages as the inhabitants gradually abandoned the maintenance of the broch towers themselves. Further south it seems that substantial roundhouses had mostly fallen out of use several centuries earlier, certainly prior to the Roman period, by which time smaller, stone-built houses were apparently the norm.

The burst of energy expended on the building of these monumental roundhouses must reflect

the nature of society at the time. After all, equally complex societies before and after the Iron Age felt no need to lavish such attention on their homes. Presumably, then, the elaboration of the house shows that the household and the domestic arena were central to the contemporary world view. As such, we should not be surprised that, as well as a place to cook, eat, sleep, work and shelter, the house could become variously a focus for religious acts, a mark of territorial or social authority, a symbol of household unity, and a place in which to meet and negotiate with neighbours and outsiders.

As in many societies today, the design of the house and the patterns of daily life within it would probably have been bound by strict social and religious codes, perhaps with areas set aside for different age or gender groups. Some such patterns emerge from the archaeological evidence. For example, the tendency for roundhouse doors to face between south and east regardless of local conditions can best be explained as reflecting widespread cosmologies (see chapter 7). Likewise, the apparent persistence of certain basic cellular or radial divisions of space across architectural traditions may be rooted in widely shared behaviour patterns, myths or modes of thought.

Despite the unique building styles that evolved in various parts of Scotland and at various times during the Iron Age, then, there are underlying patterns that seem to reflect a common cultural heritage, perhaps derived from the rather more integrated ancestral societies of the Later Bronze Age, as well as continuing contacts across Scotland and beyond. It is probably through the ever-more detailed analysis of such patterns that we have our best chance of examining the commonalities and divisions between the various tribal groups throughout Scotland in the Bronze and Iron Ages. From this we might begin to discern some trace of the shared belief systems and ethnicities that might help define a common 'Celticness'.

23 *(Overleaf)* Four stages in the construction of the wheelhouse at Cnip on the west coast of Lewis

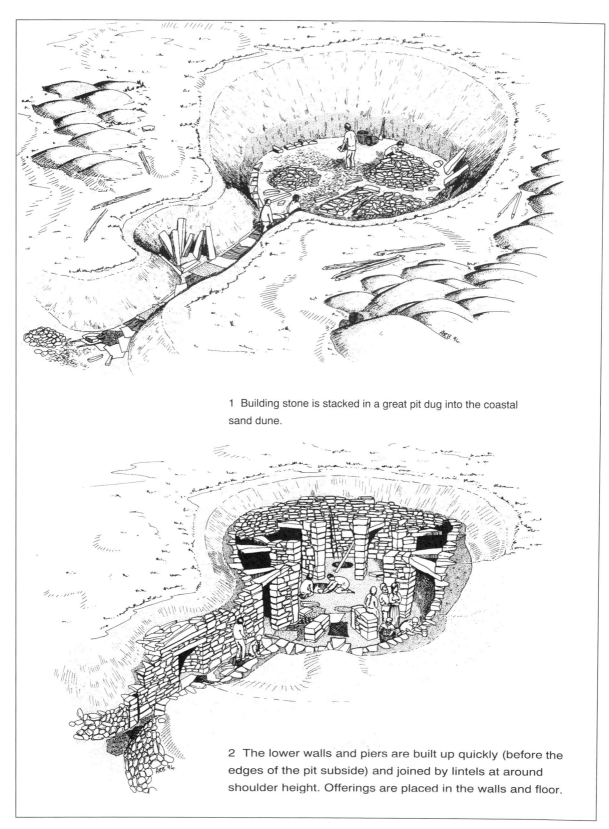

1 Building stone is stacked in a great pit dug into the coastal sand dune.

2 The lower walls and piers are built up quickly (before the edges of the pit subside) and joined by lintels at around shoulder height. Offerings are placed in the walls and floor.

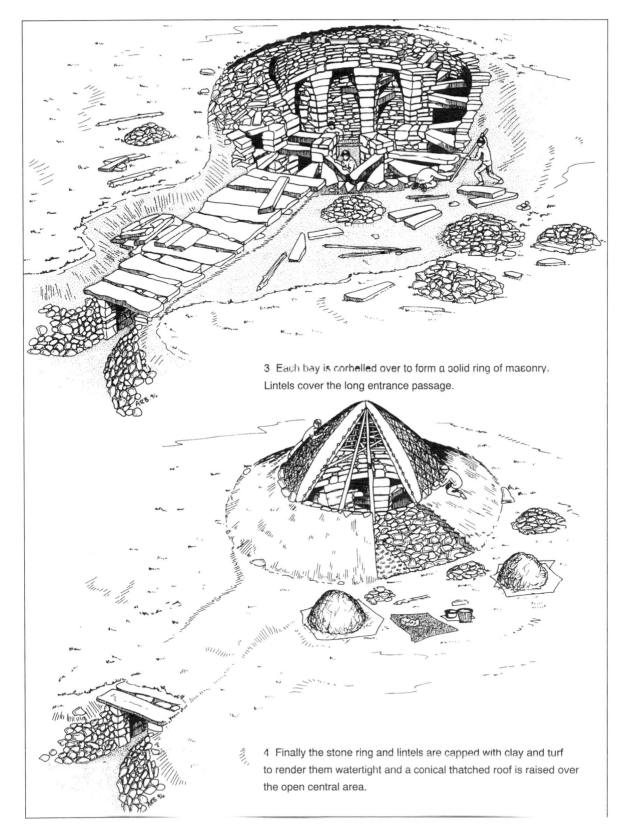

3 Each bay is corbelled over to form a solid ring of masonry.
Lintels cover the long entrance passage.

4 Finally the stone ring and lintels are capped with clay and turf
to render them watertight and a conical thatched roof is raised over
the open central area.

4
Warring Celts

Celts in conflict

Roman writers had every reason to pronounce the Celts as warlike, reckless and incapable of self-government. By doing so they could portray successive Roman advances as a positive contribution to the spread of civilized values. Archaeology has often seemed to bear out their words. After all, the classic monument of the Iron Age is surely the hillfort, stoutly defended by rampart and ditch. Indeed, this first appearance of defensive architecture was long thought to herald the arrival of Celtic migrants into Scotland. But more recent studies have shown that the defensive capabilities of such sites were often of secondary importance. As with the monumental roundhouses of the time, prestige, status or even ritual and religion could all play a part. The evolution of forts and enclosures does not, therefore, simply reflect the vagaries of warfare, but rather relates to the development of society itself.

A brief overview

Large numbers of hillforts and enclosed settlements of various forms were built over much of Scotland and northern England during the first millennium BC (**24**). Their enormous variety and the relatively small body of excavation make it difficult to discern patterns even at a very broad scale. Nonetheless, it does seem that three episodes can be discerned, even if these are poorly dated and not necessarily neatly sequential across the country.

Perhaps as early as 1000 BC a few densely (if perhaps sporadically) occupied centres had emerged, set on prominent hilltops. It seems reasonable to link these settlements with the warrior aristocracy that we see so clearly in the artefact record at around the same time. By 500

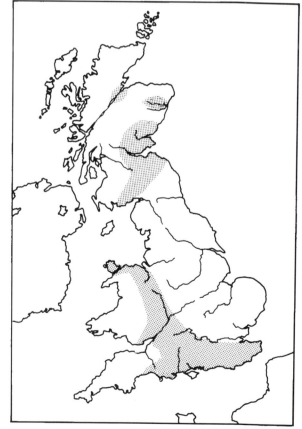

24 Hillforts are found widely across Iron Age Britain and Europe. This map shows the main concentrations in Britain.

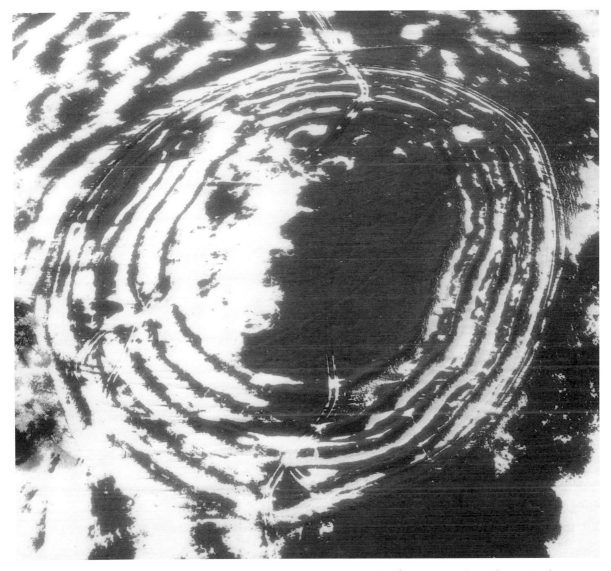

25 Corsehope Law in the Borders. A typically heavily enclosed example of the forts that crown so many southern Scottish hilltops. The sites of numerous ring-ditch houses can be dimly discerned within the interior.

BC many, generally smaller, forts and enclosures had sprung up and the earlier sites seem to have faded away, some perhaps surviving as centres of ritual importance (25). By around 200 BC most of the forts had probably ceased to function defensively, and houses spilled over the derelict ramparts. Undefended villages subsequently seem to have become more common and it was these largely open landscapes of settled farming communities that seem to have been in place immediately prior to the Roman invasion.

Within this broad pattern is immense regional and local variation. Indeed, every new hillfort excavation of any size seems to turn on its head preconceived ideas of date and development. Before looking at forts and enclosures in any more detail, however, it is useful to examine briefly the likely nature of warfare and the weapons with which it was waged.

Tribal warfare

The Roman writer Tacitus' account of the battle of Mons Graupius in AD 83 highlights some of

47

26 Swords, first of bronze then later of iron, were the favoured weapons of the elite and would have been of immense value. This example was recovered from the River Tay near Perth.

the characteristics of tribal warfare in the north. Despite cooperating to elect a single war leader, when it came to actual battle the northern tribes appear to have been ill disciplined, fighting under numerous chiefs, and using chariots to intimidate their opponents. Their inevitable slaughter cast into sharp relief the distinction between warfare as practised by tribe and state.

Even before the arrival of the Roman army, war would have been an ever-present threat to Celtic communities in Scotland, as it has been to small-scale, agricultural societies through the centuries. Yet, while it is common today to associate warfare with control of territory, land itself is worthless without the capacity to consolidate gains and maintain power. Territorial wars thus characterize states rather than tribal societies. Among these less centralized groups warfare might have taken many other forms, such as feuding or cattle raiding between neighbours, or longer-range sorties for plunder, slaves, or individual glory.

It would probably have been in the interests of Celtic chiefs or petty kings to maintain a state of perennial warfare. Such conditions would have given meaning to their own position as protectors and champions of their communities and lent a sense of cohesion and purpose to their followers. Some such 'protection rackets' could, under the right conditions, eventually develop into more cohesive political systems, such as the nascent state of Pictland in the post-Roman centuries.

The trappings of war

During the Bronze Age, increasingly efficient means of killing had been devised, principally as a result of advances in bronze-working. In the Later Bronze Age, long slashing swords of previously unparalleled viciousness were widely adopted across Europe (**26**). Some of the best Scottish examples come from the geographical periphery of the country, including bronze swords from peat bogs in Lewis, South Uist and Skye, and moulds for sword manufacture from Jarlshof in Shetland.

These swords were well suited to mounted combat and it may have been at this time that horses became more widely used for carrying warriors in battle and pulling chariots. The Scottish tribes favoured the use of chariots long after the fashion had faded elsewhere, but these may have been as much for pre-battle preening as actual fighting. These battlefield preliminaries also included the blasting of war trumpets to strike fear into the enemy. The remains of one such instrument, a boar-headed carnyx from Deskford in Banffshire (see **colour plate 5**), is a rare surviving example though similar objects are widely represented in classical coinage and sculpture as part of the paraphernalia of Celtic warfare. Before the ill-matched clash with Rome, ritualized aggression and the threat of violence may often have played as important a role as actual battles.

The iron swords that superseded the earlier bronze versions remained the favoured weapons of the elite for hundreds of years; indeed, the name of the Celtic war leader at Mons Graupius, according to Tacitus, was Calgacus, 'the swordsman'. Slings and spears would also have been used although there is, strangely perhaps, no evidence of archery and little to suggest the use of body armour. For those of lowlier station a variety of agricultural and industrial implements no doubt would have been turned to more violent use when the need arose.

The relatively small-scale nature of warfare and the strong element of display and symbolism with which it was infused must be borne in mind when we look at the hillforts. Too often these have tended to be interpreted in a rather anachronistic way, like medieval fortifications, designed to withstand siege warfare and large, well-drilled and disciplined attacking armies. Instead, it may be better to see them in the light of essentially small-scale tribal feuding, competition and confrontation.

Forts and enclosures

The hilltops, knolls and headlands of southern and eastern Scotland, and much of northern England, are littered with the desolate remains of forts and enclosures; apparently mute testimony to the violent nature of Celtic societies (27). However, to say that the Scottish Iron Age is characterized by hillforts is to simplify complex variations of geography, chronology, morphology, function and topography. Somewhere in the bewildering diversity of enclosure types one feels there must be patterns waiting to throw light on dimly

27 This distribution map of forts in Scotland is based on one compiled in 1966 with a few additions: although aerial photography has since added sites, particularly in the Lothians, the overall pattern is essentially unchanged

understood aspects of the Iron Age. Yet, despite a long tradition of excavation and survey, our knowledge of the Scottish forts remains pitifully weak, hampered by the often tiny size of excavated areas, the paucity of reliable radiocarbon dates and the meagre finds. Consequently, any attempts at understanding their development must be highly provisional.

Most excavation has taken place in the area between the Forth and the Tyne (where upwards of 90 per cent of Scottish hillforts are to be found) and this area inevitably dominates discussion, even though developments there need have little relevance to other parts of the country. While the north-east has seen some research in recent decades, the few forts of Atlantic Scotland remain largely ignored by archaeologists in favour of broch towers and related structures. Those in the south-west have fared little better.

Only a few years ago hillforts seemed to form part of a fairly straightforward sequence based on Mrs C.M. Piggott's pioneering excavations at Hownam Rings, in Roxburghshire, in 1948. Academic opinion at the time favoured the 'invasionist' view of prehistory in which changes in society were wrought by force and by the movement of populations. In this pre-radiocarbon era, the Iron Age was thought to have lasted only a few hundred years, marked by successive eruptions of continental Celts into Britain.

The sequence of occupation at Hownam Rings seemed to support this view, falling as it did into a series of well-defined phases (28). It began with a settlement surrounded by a simple palisade or timber fence. After a time this was replaced by a stone rampart and a second rampart was later added to further strengthen the defences. At length, the settlement, of stone-walled roundhouses, spread out over defences which had been allowed to fall into disrepair.

The Hownam sequence, elaborated and buttressed by work on other southern sites, seemed to provide the key to the development of Celtic society in Scotland: defences grew stronger as waves of warlike invaders, each more technologically and culturally advanced, swept across the country until, at last, the *pax Romana* enabled the essentially peaceable farmers to live unharried by hostile incomers.

However, modern excavation and the advent of radiocarbon dating have revealed a more complex situation. The period of enclosure and fortification has now been shown to extend over most, if not all, of the first millennium BC. Some forts even pre-date the conventional Iron Age and have not only their roots, but perhaps their floruit also, in the Later Bronze Age. Just as importantly, sites have now been excavated that seem to up-end the traditional sequence, the frequent changes in the scale and nature of their defences defying any simple model of development.

Eildon and Traprain – hill-towns or seasonal fairs?
Perhaps surprisingly, some of the largest hilltop enclosures appear to have been among the earliest. While most Scottish forts and enclosures are less than 1.6 hectares (4 acres) in size, a few are significantly larger, over 3.6 hectares (8.5 acres). There are next to none in between. Two of the largest, Eildon Hill North in Roxburghshire (29), and Traprain Law in East Lothian, have long been interpreted as tribal capitals or *minor oppida* of the immediately pre-Roman period (see chapter 8). Whatever the truth of this, both were also occupied much earlier.

Eildon Hill North, the highest of three hills looming over modern Melrose, has long been known to archaeologists, both for its extensive defences (some 5km (3 miles) of rampart enclosing some 16ha (40 acres) in the main phase of construction), and for the density of house platforms (an estimated 500) within them (30). Small-scale excavations have recently shown that the hilltop was probably already enclosed by around 1000 BC. Inside, platforms were scooped out of the rock to create a level surface for houses which have themselves left

28 The Hownam sequence: this classic picture of hillfort development has been shown to be an oversimplification but may still be locally applicable in the Cheviots.

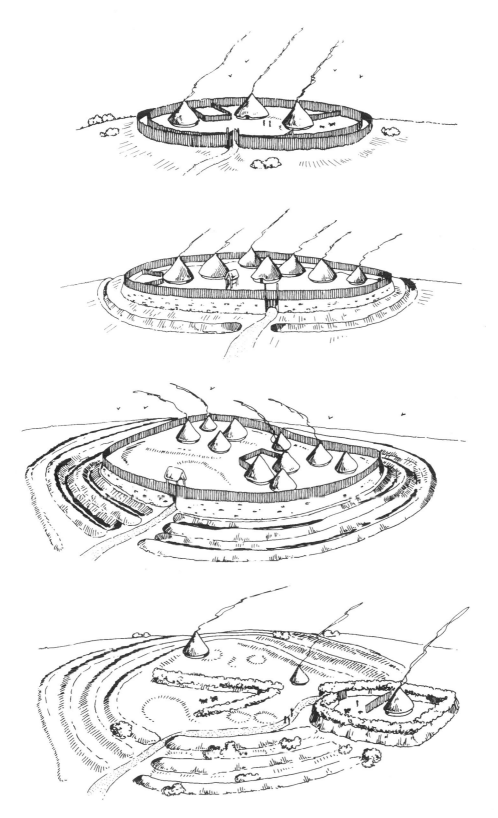

29 The hilltop enclosure of Eildon Hill North, near Melrose.

little trace. These houses may only ever have been of slight construction, although demolition and decay could account for the virtual disappearance of even quite substantial timber or turf houses.

It has been suggested that the hundreds of house platforms may have built up over many years through the repeated visits of a shifting population. This, however, seems most unlikely. Once they were built, these platforms were natural house stances for later generations. Since the construction of a second platform implies that someone was still occupying the first, the construction of several hundred implies that, at certain times, very large numbers of people were on the hill.

Another key site for the southern Scottish Iron Age is Traprain Law (**30**; and see **colour plate 6**). Despite a severe mauling by a recent quarry, this volcanic crag still dominates the fertile coastal plain of East Lothian and must always have occupied a central place in the mental geography of local inhabitants. By around 1500 BC it was already a place of burial, but by the early centuries of the first millennium BC there is evidence of settlement. The ramparts, which surround all but the craggy south face of the hill, were replaced and rebuilt on numerous occasions and, although the date of their initial construction is unknown, they may have their origins in this period. Excavations in the early decades of the twentieth century revealed numerous superimposed houses in the lower levels. Some of these seem to belong to the ring-ditch class (see chapter 3), broadly contemporary with the large quantities of Late Bronze Age metalwork and bronze-working debris from the hill.

The realization that large, densely occupied hilltop settlements like Traprain Law and Eildon Hill North had their origins as early as the Later Bronze Age, rather than the immediately pre-Roman period, is immensely significant. However, excavations on both have been minuscule relative to the size of the settlements

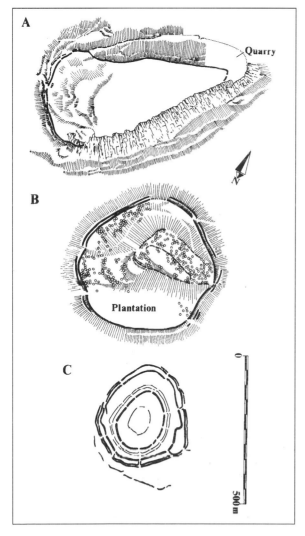

30 The origins of many large hilltop enclosures seem to lie in the Later Bronze Age: these examples are at Traprain Law, East Lothian, Eildon Hill North, Roxburghshire, and the Brown Caterthun, Angus.

themselves, and it is unsurprising that we still have little idea what they represent in terms of Later Bronze Age society. Were they perhaps hill-towns, the permanent seats of the sword-wielding aristocracy familiar from the contemporary hoards of metalwork? Clearly some individual or group must have marshalled the immense amount of labour needed to build these enclosures. Perhaps they also formed centres for the production and the distribution of specialist items like bronzework that were beyond the reach of smaller communities in the surrounding valleys and plains. It has often been suggested that the chiefs or kings of the Later Bronze Age drew much of their authority from their control of exchange, of which bronze and its raw materials, copper and tin, were a central component.

There are difficulties in interpreting these sites as purely defensive strongholds. Covering such enormous areas, the defences would have been hard to defend against determined attackers who in any case would have easily been able to observe the disposition of the defenders on the high ground within. The creation of a physical barrier to demarcate the site was possibly more important than any defensive considerations.

Perhaps, rather than 'military' strongholds, these were seasonal meeting-places, for festivals or fairs, serving large groups of people who otherwise lived in dispersed communities for most of the year: Eildon Hill North almost certainly had insufficient arable land in its immediate vicinity to feed the presumed population all year round. Ritual may have continued to play a part as it had in earlier times at Traprain. None of this need exclude the possibility that there was a small resident population, perhaps of nobility, priests or craft-workers. Symbolic defences and a ritual dimension are far from incompatible with the presence of a warrior elite; especially one engaged in ostentatious offerings of fine metalwork to the gods.

Traprain Law and Eildon Hill North, despite their prominence in the archaeological literature, were not unique. The earliest rampart around the Brown Caterthun hillfort in Angus was probably constructed between around 700–500 BC, although the hill was refortified with a more substantial wall between 500–400 BC and again a few centuries later.

Other hilltop enclosures of potentially early date include the extraordinary enclosure at Ben Griam Beg, on the Caithness–Sutherland boundary. This complex stone-walled construction, enclosing some 2.5ha (7 acres), lies at over 600m (200ft) above sea level in an environment to which the word 'hostile' can do little justice. Even in the somewhat warmer conditions of the Bronze Age it is hard to imagine that this was a simple, functional settlement or fort. The size and slight ramparts of the hilltop enclosure of White Meldon, Tweeddale, mark it as another possible early site. Both it and the enclosure on Burnswark Hill, Annandale, contain 'double ring-groove' houses, a distinctive early form of timber roundhouse dating to the early part of the first millennium BC. Many other unexcavated and undated hillforts across the country may have their origins at least as early. Indeed, large hilltop settlements seem to have been a fairly common feature in the Later Bronze Age of Ireland, Wales and the English Midlands as well as Scotland.

Yet they were not to last. By the middle of the millennium they already seem to have given way to a rather more fragmented pattern of settlement. If we are right in attributing the dense settlement of Traprain Law and Eildon Hill North to this early period, then it was to be almost 2000 years before settlements of similar size and complexity arose again.

Changing patterns of enclosure

With the collapse of exchange systems based on the bronze industry, individual communities seem to have become much more inward-looking and self-sufficient. Iron was much easier to come by and thus more difficult for a small group of people to control. Whatever trade networks or craft specialization had existed in

31 The photograph above shows palisade trenches under excavation at the site of Myrehead, near Falkirk. Upright timbers would originally have been bedded in the trenches and packed in with small stones. The photograph opposite shows the settlement at Harehope in the Borders: the banks each supported a palisade, surrounding a central roundhouse.

the Later Bronze Age began to break down. But even before the introduction of iron many smaller forts and enclosures had begun to appear.

Palisaded enclosures Small enclosed settlements had thrived for some time in the shadow of the larger centres. Some of the earliest, from around 800 BC, were defined by timber palisades and often contained one or more ring-ditch houses (like those discussed in chapter 3). Remarkably, the narrow bedding trenches dug to hold the timbers of the palisades can sometimes still be seen as shallow grooves in the ground surface, particularly in the upland pastures of the Cheviots (31).

At Dryburn Bridge, in East Lothian, a palisaded enclosure surrounding a substantial timber roundhouse was built around 750 BC (32).

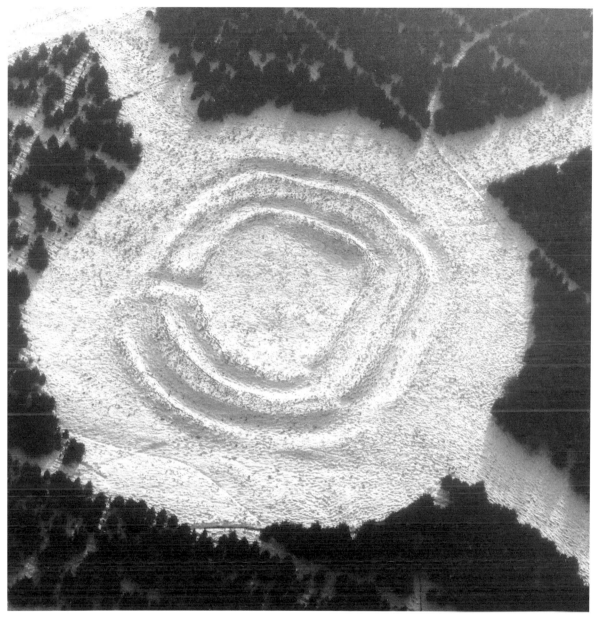

Subsequently, a number of ring-ditch houses were built in and around the enclosure. The excavator has interpreted these remains as signifying the replacement of an original palisaded homestead containing one principal house by an unenclosed village, a sequence that confounds the expectations of the conventional Hownam sequence, where the trend ought to be towards even heavier enclosure.

Many palisaded enclosures, like those at Hownam Rings and Burnswark Hill, were subsequently replaced by more substantial ramparts of stone and earth, while others were either abandoned or persisted as unenclosed settlements. Indeed, although palisaded enclosures continued to be built into the Early Historic period, there is a tendency for them to represent the first phase of settlement on any given site. Perhaps it was simply the availability of timber, cleared from the land when settlements were first established, that encouraged the construction of timber rather than stone or earth enclosures.

32 This aerial view of Dryburn Bridge in East Lothian, shows the large palisaded enclosure under excavation; the remains of several ring-ditch houses are clearly visible both within and outside the enclosure.

Forts The complexity of Iron Age forts in Scotland has been highlighted by the near-total excavation of a cropmark fort at Broxmouth in East Lothian (**33**). Excavations here in advance of quarrying in the late 1970s revealed a sequence of enclosure that defied any expected progression from simple to elaborate. During the early part of the first millennium BC, an unenclosed settlement, focused on a large timber roundhouse, occupied the low hill. By around 700 BC the settlement had been enclosed by first one and then a second rampart and ditch. So far, this would appear to follow the expected trajectory of development towards ever more impregnable defence. But in the case of Broxmouth this bi-vallate fort was remodelled with a single rampart. Further rebuildings followed, interspersed with periods of decay of the defences, until finally, around 200 BC, an unenclosed settlement of stone-walled roundhouses occupied the site of the derelict ramparts.

It was the scale of the excavations at Broxmouth that permitted the unravelling of this tangled sequence. When one considers the keyhole trenches that form much of evidence for Scottish forts, it seems almost inevitable that the complexity of many previously excavated sites has been grossly underestimated, although surface traces of overlapping ramparts, as at Barry Hill in Perthshire (see **colour plate 7**), betray the time-depth on some sites.

Although centuries of ploughing had all but removed the ramparts at Broxmouth, the details

of rampart structure often survive on upland sites. Perhaps the most overtly militaristic were those enclosed by stone walls bolstered by an internal structure of substantial, horizontal timbers. Professor Childe's excavations at Abernethy hillfort, in Perthshire, produced impressive evidence of a stone-faced rampart with holes which originally held timbers (**34**). The coastal fort of Cullykhan in Banffshire had an additional series of timber uprights along its

33 The deep, wide ditches around many ploughed-out forts and settlements can produce well-defined cropmarks. This site at Broxmouth in East Lothian produced a wealth of evidence for Iron Age settlement.

34 This photograph was taken during early excavations on Abernethy hillfort in Perthshire. The gaps in the stone face of the rampart show where timbers would once have projected.

face, possibly in place of a stone-faced wall. Cullykhan also produced evidence of a massively built entrance passage flanked by large posts, suggesting a rather imposing approach to the fort. Childe's excavations at Finavon in Angus revealed that the timber-laced wall on that site would have stood to a height of around 6m (18ft), another extremely intimidating construction.

These timber-laced forts, once thought to have been a continental innovation close to the time of the Roman invasions, have been shown by radiocarbon dating to have been built, albeit discontinuously, from around 700 BC through to the Early Historic period. In fact, some Scottish examples are actually many centuries earlier than their supposed continental prototypes. In particular, French timber-laced forts held together with long iron nails seem not to have

been built more than a century or so before the Caesarean invasion and were probably unconnected with prehistoric timber-laced forts in Scotland. So far, iron-nailed timber-lacing has only been found on later, Pictish period fortifications in Scotland, as at Burghead in Moray and Dundurn in Perthshire.

At Burnswark Hill a rampart dating to around the sixth century BC had a skeleton of both vertical and horizontal timbers, forming a box-like construction. Although widespread in southern England, this technique is so far unique in Scotland where the ready availability of stone for rampart facings made vertical timbers redundant (although close-spaced timber palisades may in some cases represent a framework for a similar, box-like construction). At Burnswark it seems that stylistic or cultural considerations determined that the rampart should be built like those far to the south. Indeed, Barry Cunliffe has said that it would 'not be out of place in Hampshire or Dorset'; a rare archaeological illustration of the kind of exchange of ideas that might have been brought about through military alliance, inter-marriage, or long-distance trade.

Vitrified forts In a number of cases, as at Finavon, timber-laced forts met their ends by burning under conditions of such extreme heat that the stone and earth melted and fused, or 'vitrified', to produce a hard, glassy mass (a phenomenon also encountered in parts of France where the geology is appropriate). Even at Broxmouth, where the ramparts were all but gone, traces of vitrified gravel suggest that the ramparts there had undergone a similar process.

It was once thought that these vitrified forts had been either fired deliberately to provide extra strength or that they had been burned in the course of battle. In fact, neither of these explanations works: vitrification of the wall core would not have added any strength to the rampart but rather would have weakened it, while the temperatures needed to produce vitrification are such that casual or opportunistic fires, started in battle, would have been insufficient.

Experiments have shown that only deliberately maintained fires, demanding perseverance and copious quantities of fuel could have produced the right conditions unless the wall was tinder dry. Vitrification was thus not simply a by-product of war, but rather a premeditated act of intense symbolic power as the seats of a warrior aristocracy were permanently and spectacularly razed.

Promontory forts In many cases the natural topography of coastal headlands and inland promontories provided ready-made defensible locations. Promontory forts are particularly characteristic of the northern coasts and represent probably the largest group of forts in the Northern and Western Isles. In these areas there are obvious architectural relationships between promontory forts and broch architecture (see chapter 3). The example at Barra Head, on Berneray in the Western Isles, incorporates superimposed galleries within a wall some 5m (16ft) wide across the neck of an exposed coastal promontory. Its low entrance with bar-holes for a wooden door are strikingly similar to those of the Atlantic roundhouses.

Numerous promontory forts are also found along the east coast, north of the Forth. These sites, defended by one or more ramparts, range in date from the mid-first millennium BC to the historical Pictish period. Some, including the fort at Cullykan in Banffshire, were in use for many centuries. The massive promontory fort of Burghead, in Moray, seems to have been an important Pictish naval base and perhaps a royal centre in the Early Historic period. Perhaps other promontory forts played an equally important naval role in the pre-Roman period.

Stronghold or symbol?
The use of terms like hillfort and promontory fort implies that we know what these sites represent; military structures built by strutting conquerors or nervous natives in times of unrest and change. Yet we have already seen how some early hilltop enclosures were defined only by slight walls or terraces that might merely accentuate the natural contours. These were more likely places of communal gathering or religious significance, perhaps with a small resident population. For some of the smaller forts and enclosures, too, there are reasons to believe that defence may not have been the sole or even principal consideration.

The Chesters, sitting amid a heavily settled and extensively cultivated landscape (see chapter 5) near Drem in East Lothian, is a prime example of a defensively ineffectual fort (see **colour plate 8**). The adjacent high ridge, as well as making a fine platform from which to view the multiple ramparts, would have been an eminently suitable place from which to rain down missiles on the fort's defenders. Yet the investment of labour represented by its ramparts must have been spent to some purpose; in this case presumably the glorification of the fort's inhabitants.

Even more effort was expended on the twin hillforts of the White and Brown Caterthun (35). These massive multi-period constructions overlook vast tracts of Strathmore in Angus yet, rather than exploiting the defensive qualities of

35 This artist's impression shows building works in progress on the second phase ramparts at the Brown Caterthun in Angus, some time between 500 and 400 BC. By this time the earlier ramparts slightly further down the hill had probably fallen into disrepair.

their hilltop locations, their multiple entrances (there are nine on the Brown Caterthun) seem to invite access from the valleys below.

On some very large sites, like Traprain Law or Eildon Hill North, it is easy to imagine that the hilltops might at one time have housed all of those who took part in its construction, although presumably the coordination of the work involved implies strong leadership and hierarchies of some form. The same is true of some palisaded settlements where smaller communities might have banded together to enclose their villages. But on small, heavily enclosed forts, like the Chesters and Broxmouth, the scale of the enclosing works seem out of all proportion to the size of the interior.

At Broxmouth, for example, it has been calculated that just one of the enclosure ditches represented around two months' continuous work for a team of around seventy men. This takes no account of the accompanying rampart which may have required even more work, particularly if stone and timber had to be won and transported to the site. Unless they were built over a considerable number of years, many more people would seem to have been involved in the construction process than were ever invited to live within the walls (**36**).

We can recognize a site like the Chesters as a symbol of power rather than a military stronghold because of its topographical setting. Elsewhere, however, defence and prestige can be hard to tell apart. Elaborate gateways, for example, might be designed either to impress outsiders entering the settlement (**37** and **38**), or to strengthen defensive weak points (or both). Forts may be set on hills to help them repel or attack, or because the occupants wanted physical dominance of the surrounding landscape.

These different motives may find some reflection in the strikingly different ways in which forts and enclosures occupy different landscapes across Scotland. East Lothian and Tweeddale, for example, are so crowded with enclosures that it is hard to believe that they could all have been home to high-ranking families: indeed, it is possible that the majority of the rural population may have occupied such settlements (**39** and **40**). Here, there seems to have existed a rather fragmented society where considerable independence was exercised locally and where small communities or clans competed for resources and stamped their own mark, in the form of an enclosed settlement, however modest, on their patch of land. Often these enclosures may have been defined by very slight ditches and simple dump ramparts, some perhaps forming the base of impenetrable hedgerows rather than formal defences.

North of the Tay is a very different picture. In Strathmore and the Lunan Valley, for example,

open settlements of roundhouses and souterrains sprawl over substantial tracts of arable land, while the few hillforts perch in commanding positions overlooking the fertile lowlands. Villagers and farmers from the valleys must have laboured long and hard on these hillfort defences, presumably as part of the homage paid to their social superiors in a rather more overtly ranked society than we see further south.

36 At Dodridge Law, in East Lothian, the scale of the defensive works, visible as cropmark ditches, seem out of all reasonable proportion to the small area enclosed. Presumably the defences here were built by people from lesser settlements in the surrounding area. The constant upkeep and repair of the ramparts and the periodic acts of reconstruction and remodelling that form the 'phases' of our archaeological excavations would have continued to restate these relationships of equality or dominance down the generations. Perhaps some of the great hillfort reconstructions represent the coming to power of new chiefs or kings, keen to legitimize their position by maintaining and improving on the works of their predecessors.

37 *(Left)* The enclosed settlement at Old Montrose in Angus is shown here as a cropmark. The two parallel ditches leading off from the enclosure (at the top of the photograph) are part of a much earlier 'cursus' monument; a ritual avenue of the Neolithic period.

38 *(Below)* A reconstruction of the Old Montrose settlement shows how the deliberate choice of siting, at the end of cursus, created a monumental approach to an otherwise run-of-the-mill settlement.

39 *(Opposite)* These two maps show the distribution of enclosed settlements around Traprain Law. In the first only upstanding sites are shown. The second shows the vast increase in numbers when the cropmark sites are added.

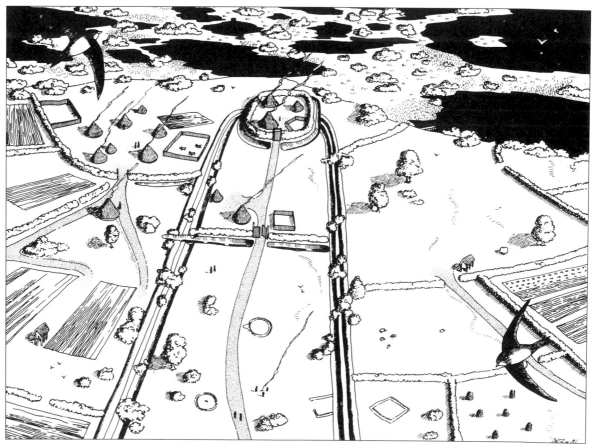

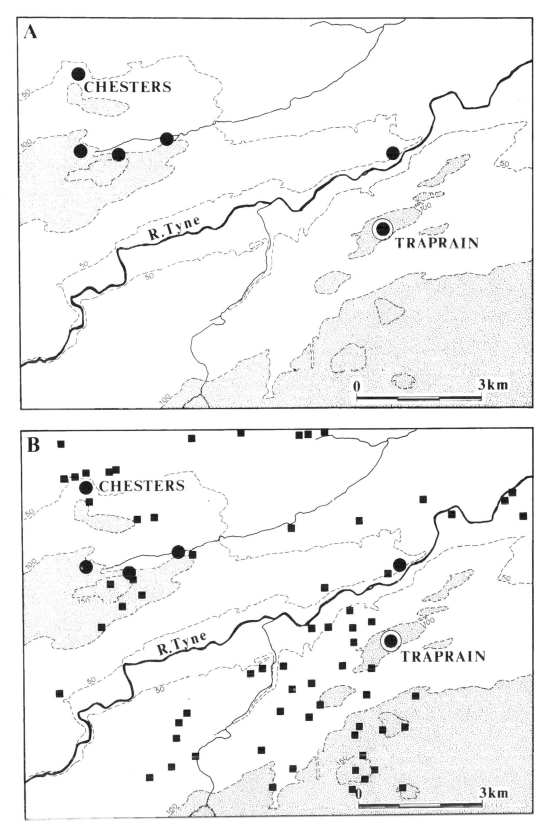

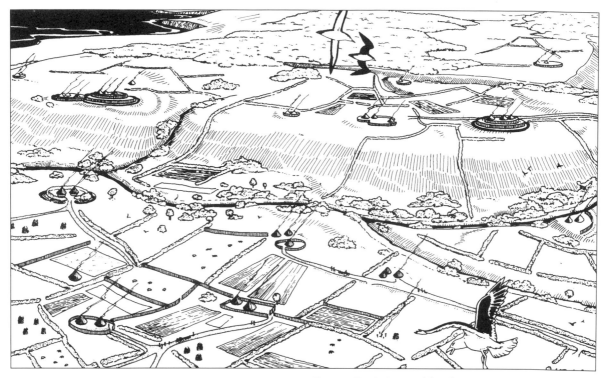

40 Some parts of south-east Scotland were densely settled by communities living in enclosed settlements of various forms. Because many of these settlements were sited so prominently, the countryside might have seemed considerably more crowded than it is today. This artist's impression gives some idea of the way the landscape of East Lothian might have looked around 500 BC.

Instances where one can suggest direct contact between Scottish tribal leaders and their geographically distant peers form no coherent pattern. The apparently alien and Wessex-like ramparts at Burnswark Hill in the south-west have already been mentioned. Another tangible, if rather enigmatic, manifestation of long-distance contacts is the sporadic occurrence in Scotland of stone *chevaux-de-frise*: upright stones densely set in the ground to impede access. Timber *chevaux-de-frise* seem to have first appeared in Central Europe during the Later Bronze Age as a means of repulsing attacks by mounted warriors. Their stone counterparts have been identified only in Iberia, Ireland, Wales and Scotland, where the motley and scattered examples range from the fort of

Dreva Craig in Peeblesshire to Burgi Geos, a stone blockhouse in Shetland some 500km (300miles) away. In keeping with the defensive ineptitude of so many Scottish forts, the *chevaux-de-frise* at Burgi Geos, far from blocking access, seem rather to line the path to the site, suggesting that the blockhouse-dwellers wanted to invoke the exotic and militaristic connotations of the technique without the associated inconvenience; perhaps not unlike the owners of nineteenth-century baronial 'castles'.

Disuse and desertion

The abandonment of forts used to be regarded, quite reasonably, as the direct result of the Roman invasion. Following Mons Graupius, the Scottish tribes were effectively demilitarized. Under this *pax Romana* small farming settlements of 'Votadinian' houses (see chapter 8) were thought to have crept over the disused walls of many southern forts. In the Cheviots small, enclosed, but hardly defensive, farmsteads emerged, characterized by groups of these stone-built houses set around a sunken yard.

1 A reconstruction of a hut circle settlement in Holyrood Park, Edinburgh

2 Dun Carloway, broch tower, Lewis

3 Gurness, broch tower and village, Orkney, from the air   4 A reconstruction of the broch village at Gurness, in Orkney

5 A reconstruction of the Deskford carnyx in use

6 Traprain Law, East Lothian

7 The fort on Barry Hill, Angus

8 The Chesters fort, in East Lothian

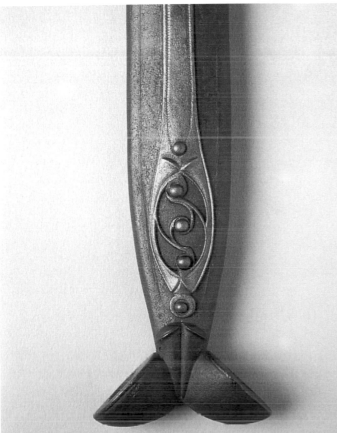

9 Iron Age cultivation of freely draining slopes in Holyrood Park. The remains of such terraces are clearly visible in the park even today

10 The Mortonhall scabbard

11 Detail from the terminal of a gold torc from Shaw Hill, Peeblesshire

12 The Balmaclellan mirror

13 A scene from the Column of Marcus in Rome, showing Roman soldiers torching a native village during the campaigns of Marcus Aurelius (AD 161–180), north of the River Danube

14 The broch and surrounding settlement at Edin's Hall in the Borders

15 A gilt silver flask from the Traprain Law hoard

However, radiocarbon dating has now placed the abandonment of some Iron Age fortifications rather earlier. At Broxmouth, for example, the stone-walled 'Votadinian' houses began to appear as early as the second century BC, after the inhabitants had ceased to maintain their elaborate defences. The scatter of hillforts in Argyll and the rest of Atlantic Scotland, such as Balloch Hill and Dun Lagaidh, seem also to have been succeeded by smaller, scattered settlements of Atlantic roundhouse type by the later centuries BC.

While their defences were often slighted, the sites of many forts continued in occupation well into the first century AD. Indeed, it has been estimated that around 20 per cent of upland hillforts were occupied on the eve of the Roman invasion. There may also have been a trend towards smaller stone-built forts in the later centuries BC. One such site, at Brough Law in Northumberland, dating to around 300 BC, has similarities to smaller forts in southern Scotland such as Dreva Craig, Peeblesshire and Dalmahoy, Midlothian. It may be possible to discern a pattern of divergence between forts that were replaced by apparently lower status undefended farms, and those that became the strongholds of the warrior elite, such as Turin Hill in Angus, where the hillfort was replaced by smaller stone-built 'duns'. Open farming settlements dating to the immediately pre-Roman period have been found at sites like New Mains and probably also Inveresk, in the formerly hillfort and enclosure-dominated landscapes of East Lothian. This pattern, however vaguely defined at present, may reflect a trend towards centralization of authority under fewer but more powerful chiefs, much as we see in the Atlantic north and west with the emergence of broch villages and wheelhouses.

Rather ironically, in view of Roman testimony to the ferocity and instability of Celtic society, the archaeological evidence suggests that, in the immediately pre-invasion period, the indigenous populations of Scotland were enjoying their most peaceful and prosperous period for several centuries. Landscapes formerly crowded with hillforts and enclosures appear to have been replaced by more open settlements and signs of increasingly stable conditions, while the anarchic pattern of early Atlantic roundhouse settlement in the north and west had settled down in a similar way.

5
'Celtic cowboys' and the myth of Caledon

In 1968 Professor Stuart Piggott characterized the peoples of the Scottish Iron Age as 'Celtic cowboys ... footloose and unpredictable'. Their pastoral, possibly nomadic, life-style was expressed as a direct contrast to the agricultural economies of southern England where grain storage pits, granaries and fields, the paraphernalia of settled farmers, were more obvious. This view reflected the powerful influence of the classical texts: Cassius Dio, writing around AD 220, had condemned the northern tribes as having no 'cultivated lands, but living by pastoral pursuits and by hunting, and on certain kinds of berries', adding for good measure that they lived naked, barefoot and in tents.

Since Piggott made his much-quoted statement a mass of new data has become available. Aerial photography has brought to light extensive landscapes of buried lowland settlement, while traces of cultivation have been found in the uplands at altitudes once unthinkable for the Iron Age. These discoveries force us to rethink the old picture of a heavily forested country where a small and dispersed population roamed with their flocks and herds. Instead, we have to imagine crowded lowland landscapes of fields, pasture, wetlands and managed woodland, and the periodic expansion of settlers into the upland pastures. Indeed, the first such expansion pre-dates the Iron Age by several centuries and seems to have taken place in the middle of the second millennium BC (**41**).

The Bronze Age crash

The Later Bronze Age is usually regarded as a period of environmental and economic decline. From around 1300 BC the climate seems to have become gradually colder and wetter, to such an extent that communities in some marginal lands were forced to give up agriculture altogether. As a result, extensive Bronze Age landscapes survive in some parts of the British Isles, for example on Dartmoor, and in parts of Shetland, where the abandoned lands were never reclaimed.

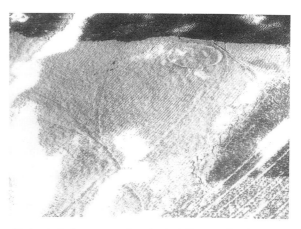

41 A relatively recent archaeological discovery has been the survival of cord rig; narrow, spade-dug cultivation ridges 1–1.5m (3–3½ft) apart running up and downslope to aid drainage. Cord rig plots were cultivated at Achany Glen, Lairg, as early as 1500 BC and survive elsewhere throughout the first millennium BC and later. A light covering of snow shows up fields of cord rig here at Orchard Rig in Peeblesshire, where they overlie an earlier palisaded enclosure.

This retreat from the uplands seems to be mirrored in many parts of Scotland. On the Hebridean island of North Uist, farmers abandoned the interior of the island as peat encroached and soils became degraded. In Achany Glen, near Lairg in Sutherland, peat growth and podsolization of the soils seems to have forced farmers off the uplands for several centuries from around 1000 BC. The next 500 years then saw the re-emergence of the 'wildscape' with species like oak reappearing after an absence of many centuries.

Often these marginal communities seem to have played a significant part in their own downfall: excessive cultivation over the centuries had exhausted many upland soils and, when combined with over-zealous clearance of trees and relentless grazing, this made them vulnerable to catastrophic erosion. However, some factors were beyond any human influence. Studies of the rings in ancient Irish oaks have shown periods of stunted growth that can be related to catastrophic volcanic eruptions in Iceland.

The dust clouds and sulphur dioxide thrown up by volcanoes can have dramatic climatic effects over the whole hemisphere, causing general cooling and local extremes of weather. Attempts have even been made to correlate historical accounts of such volcanic effects from areas as far apart as China, Rome and Ireland in the years around 207 BC and AD 540. In each case the result was widespread famine with knock-on effects of disease and social dislocation.

The eruption of the Icelandic volcano Hekla in 1159 BC seems to have had the most profound effects on the Irish climate (the beleaguered Irish oaks took eighteen years to recover) and there can be little doubt that Scotland would have suffered similar problems. It has even been suggested that related climatic effects could have played a part in the downfall of contemporary Mycenaean and Chinese civilizations. It is tempting, therefore, to link this event and its aftermath with the Later Bronze Age retreat from the uplands.

Iron Age farmers in the lowlands

Despite this rather apocalyptic vision of economic devastation in the Highlands and Islands, there is little matching evidence in the south and east of the country. Indeed, what was going on in the Scottish lowlands in the centuries from around 1500 to 1000 BC remains something of a mystery, since centuries of merciless ploughing have scoured away all but the most indelible settlement traces.

Many areas of good modern farmland would have been out of bounds to prehistoric farmers: some heavy soils could not have been cultivated before the advent of iron tools, while bad drainage prevented agriculture over large tracts of lowland Scotland until the improvements of recent centuries. Nonetheless, in favourable areas prehistoric exploitation would have been far more intensive than in the uplands, where archaeological sites tend to be best preserved. The very fact that substantial numbers of people had established farms in the apparently unpromising uplands suggests that the more fertile lowlands were already occupied close to capacity.

There can be little doubt that lowland settlement was based on a mixed economy in which arable agriculture played a central role. This is clear partly from the density of settlements in areas like East Lothian, north-east Fife and Angus, where they are found as cropmarks, and partly from finds of querns for grinding grain, and charred traces of the crops themselves, mostly barley with some wheat and oats.

It should be no surprise that settlement and cultivation were widespread. After all, Tacitus claimed that 30,000 Celts fought at Mons Graupius, and this force was apparently drawn largely from 'less favoured' northern regions. A conservative estimate of the number of house platforms originally present on Eildon Hill North would be about 500. It has been estimated that if they were all were inhabited at one time (and why build a new platform if another is free?) there may have been upwards of 3000 people on the site. The much smaller fort at Broxmouth in East Lothian may have

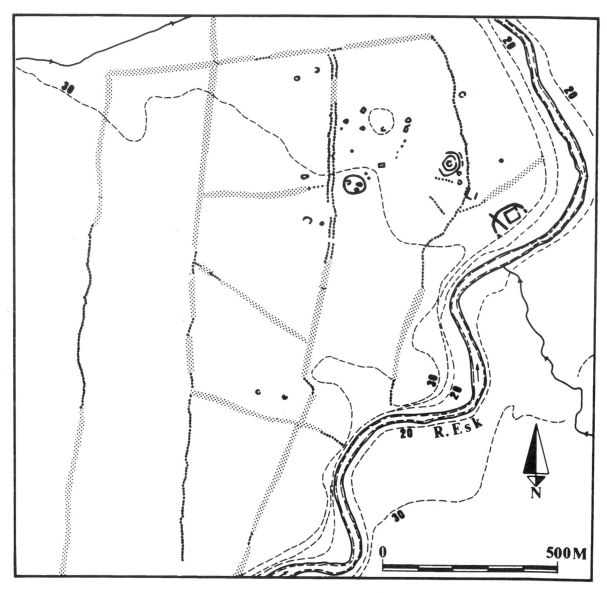

42 The landscape around Castlesteads in East Lothian was divided into long pit-defined fields interspersed with enclosures and roundhouses, all recorded as cropmarks. The dark features indicate the known cropmarks; the lighter lines represent an attempt to recreate the original layout of the fields by 'joining the dots'.

housed around 250–300 people, based on the density of houses. Given the numbers of such forts, and bearing in mind that Broxmouth is by no means exceptional, the population must have been substantial and heavy demands would have been made on arable and grazing lands. An estimate of 30–40 families occupying the broch village at Gurness in Orkney has similar implications for the Northern Isles.

Landscapes and boundaries in the lowlands
One of the most important discoveries made through aerial photography in the lowlands has been the identification of extensive field systems apparently associated with prehistoric settlements. At Castlesteads in the Esk Valley, just east of Edinburgh, a series of long fields defined by alignments of substantial pits encloses at least 150 hectares (375 acres) of prime arable land (**42**). A

similar scale of landscape division can be seen around the upstanding fort of The Chesters, near Drem in East Lothian (see **colour plate 8**), where again lines of pits divide up substantial tracts of lowland arable land. Although it is notoriously difficult to date these boundaries, there is some evidence that these rich lowlands were formally apportioned during the Iron Age, since both the Castlesteads and Chesters complexes are peppered with cropmarks of distinctive Iron Age settlements.

These pit-boundaries probably acted to prevent potentially disastrous encounters between stock and crops, but there is little agreement among archaeologists as to the precise form they took. The large pits may have held posts, perhaps supporting hurdle fences, or, more likely, they may simply have served as quarry pits for a bank that has long since been ploughed flat. Such a bank may have served as a foundation for a hedgerow or fence.

Despite the widespread occurrence of pit alignments, recognizable lowland field systems remain rare. Fields divided into small rectangular plots have been identified in the environs of Roman forts, such as Carriden (**43**), at the east end of the Antonine Wall, and Inveresk, Musselburgh, but these probably represent some form of allotment associated with the Roman army and its entourage, rather than manifestations of an indigenous system.

Grain storage and surplus
North of the Forth there are no obvious equivalents of the Castlesteads or Chesters landscapes but the dense spreads of timber roundhouses surviving as cropmarks in areas like north-east Fife, and the Lunan Valley in

43 The field system outside the Roman fort at Carriden, near Bo'ness, consists of small enclosures unrepresentative of native farming practices.

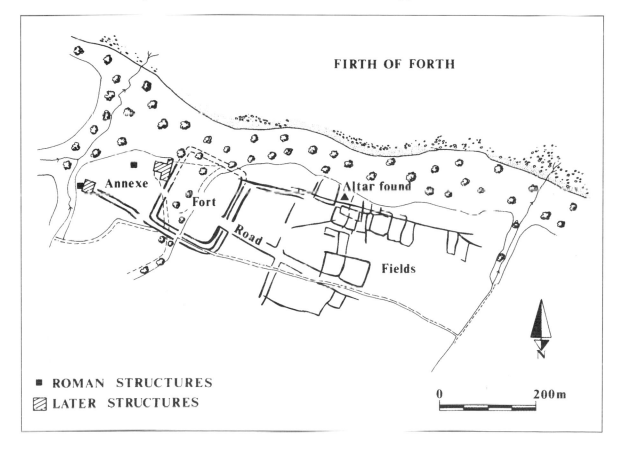

FIRTH OF FORTH

Annexe

Fort

Altar found

Road

Fields

N

■ ROMAN STRUCTURES

▨ LATER STRUCTURES

0   200m

Angus, show that Iron Age settlement was just as intense (**44**). Dotted among these settlements are numerous examples of one of the most common, yet enigmatic of Iron Age monuments: the souterrain or 'earth house'.

Souterrains were cellars, built partly or wholly underground, often entered from timber or stone roundhouses (**45**). None of the many theories on their use is entirely satisfactory and in all likelihood these semi-underground passages probably served different purposes in different times and places. They were once thought to be refuges in times of war, but their visibility above ground would have made them death traps for anyone hiding inside. They could not have been byres, since their entrances often seem almost purpose-built to hamper access for

people, let alone stock. Although entered from houses, they were not themselves apparently inhabited, while the lack of light and air would have prevented their use as industrial workshops (although some were used for this purpose after they had fallen into disrepair and were perhaps no longer fully roofed).

It has been suggested that souterrains served some ritual purpose, although this seems to be based largely on the lack of other convincing explanations, rather than on anything positive. However, nothing in the Iron Age seems to have been entirely without a ritual dimension and the role of souterrains in Iron Age religion will be discussed further in chapter 7. The interpretation with the widest applicability, though, is that they were used for storage of agricultural products: the cool, dry conditions and easily controlled access would have made them secure cellars for grain, milk and cheese. However, that this explanation cannot be universally applied is

44 Part of a cropmark landscape near Leuchars in Fife. The dark circles represent the remains of timber roundhouses preserved under the ploughsoil.

proved by the Tungadale souterrain in Skye which sits obstinately, collecting water, at the base of a hillslope.

The storage theory is an appealing explanation, at least for the large southern souterrains, as it appears to fill an otherwise surprising gap in the Scottish archaeological record. 'Four-posters', probable granary buildings set on stout timbers, have been identified on numerous excavated sites in southern Scotland, such as the enclosed settlements of Broxmouth and Dryburn Bridge in East Lothian and unenclosed settlements such as Douglasmuir and Ironshill in Angus, but nowhere do we see the sorts of concentration that have led to the interpretation of some southern English hillforts

45 Souterrains range from massive subterranean chambers like this one at Newmill in Perthshire (shown during excavation) to the rather poky tunnels of the Northern Isles. Similar structures have been found as far afield as Brittany, Cornwall and Ireland.

as centres for the collection and redistribution of grain. Souterrains may help to fill this otherwise rather puzzling gap.

The earliest known souterrains in mainland Scotland are a group of timber-walled examples from Dalladies in Grampian, which date to the third century BC, while the stone-walled example at Newmill in Perthshire was probably built in the first century BC (see 45). This dating, together with the density of souterrains in areas

like Angus, seems to show that a considerable surplus of grain was being generated by lowland farmers several centuries prior to the Roman invasion (**46**). What we do not yet know, however, is who was responsible for storing this grain and whether it was collected to accumulate individual wealth, to give to the gods, or for communal redistribution. However, the sheer numbers of souterrains in areas like Angus imply that they served small communities or villages rather than being restricted to high-status centres (**47**).

Souterrains remained in use well into the first two centuries AD. One at Crichton in Midlothian was certainly built no earlier than

46 The intensification of agriculture in the last few centuries BC is reflected in the change from traditional saddle querns, simple hollowed stones in which the grain was ground manually, to more sophisticated rotary querns. This change seems to have occurred in southern Scotland around the third century BC as it did elsewhere in northern and western Europe. This drawing shows a rotary quern in use.

47 This drawing shows the construction of the souterrain complex at Pitcur in Perthshire. The souterrains are shown as cellars leading off above-ground timber roundhouses.

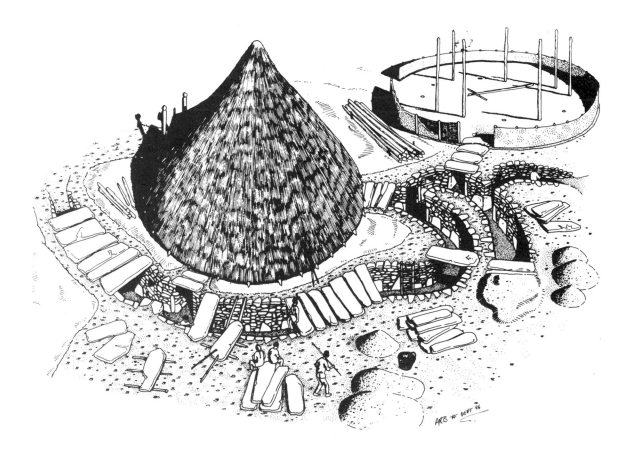

around AD 150, since Roman dressed stones (including one with a carved Pegasus, the emblem of a Roman legion) had been used in the walls and roof (48). A massively built souterrain dug into the silted-up ditch of Castlelaw fort in the Pentland Hills may be equally late. However, the ubiquitous Roman finds in many souterrains could have accumulated when they were roofless ruins and need not always indicate a late date. The reasons for their final abandonment remain obscure: perhaps they were replaced by above-ground barns or by centralized stores controlled by the elites of the emergent post-Roman kingdoms.

Herds and flocks

Despite the evidence for arable agriculture many communities probably remained dependent to a greater or lesser extent on stock-rearing. In the lowlands, cattle, probably kept mainly for meat since there is little evidence for dairying, predominated over sheep and pigs. However, bone rarely survives on lowland sites and most of our evidence for pastoralism tends to come from the north and west.

In the Western Isles, animal husbandry did not always reflect the best use of the local environment. The inhabitants of the Cnip wheelhouse in Lewis, for example, although they did raise some sheep, chose to keep a great many cattle even though the poor local grazing meant that these were rather stunted and miserable creatures. Yet even these, it seems, were more prized than the sheep that would otherwise have thrived on these lands, a Hebridean reflection perhaps of the status accorded to cattle-ownership in the Irish literary sources.

Cnip also provided evidence for the management of red deer for meat, hides and antlers. There is similar evidence from Dun Mor Vaul on Tiree, despite the complete unsuitability of that small island for the co-existence of humans and wild deer herds: again, there must have been a significant element of management. Deer are also the only type of animal depicted

on Scottish Iron Age pottery, and a fine wooden handle carved with a deer's head has been found in the waterlogged midden of Dun Bharabhat in Lewis. Interestingly, deer are also the sole animal to feature on continental painted pottery of the same broad period. It is tempting to suggest that deer were exploited for their status associations rather than for any rational economic reasons.

We need many more well-studied animal bone assemblages before firm conclusions can be drawn, but already we may be seeing glimmers of the ways in which prestige and social status influenced what we might expect to be basic economic strategies.

Hunting and gathering , fishing and fowling

In the lowlands there were probably few deer left by the Iron Age and even the substantial animal bone assemblage from Broxmouth shows negligible evidence of hunting or even fishing. But even in these farming lands wild plants, berries, nuts, seeds, fruit, herbs and fungi would have been collected for food, drink, flavourings and medicines, although these are notoriously difficult to detect archaeologically.

The Hebridean wheelhouses give some indication of the variety of birds and fish that would have been exploited by coastal communities throughout Scotland. Cnip and Sollas produced the remains of numerous sea-birds: the shag, great auk (now extinct), guillemot, puffin, gannet, migratory goose and diver. They also yielded fish: hake, saithe, cod and ballan wrasse, some species requiring deep-sea fishing. Shellfish, too, were a staple food, and were probably also used as bait. In these island communities marine mammals, such as seals, were hunted, while stranded whales provided occasional but welcome windfalls, yielding meat, oil and bones for tools and fuel.

Nonetheless, by the first millennium BC there can have been few communities relying for their basic dietary needs on purely wild resources, and in some areas hunting may already have become an exclusive pursuit for the wealthy,

48 The souterrain at Crichton is remarkably well preserved with its original roof virtually intact. This structure was built partly with dressed Roman building stone and probably dates to around 150 BC. One of the roofing slabs depicts an incomplete pegasus; the emblem of a Roman legion (right).

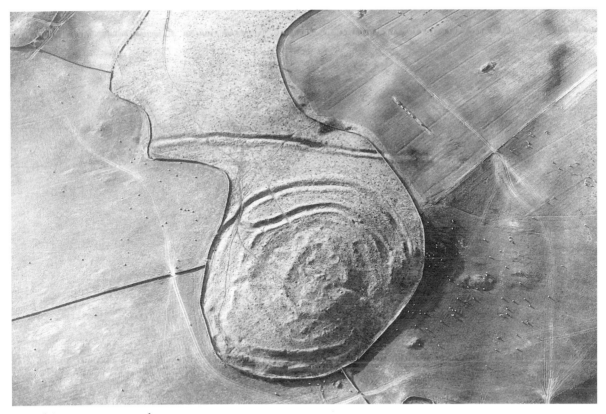

Breaking new ground

We are still some way from being able to date the period of agricultural intensification that led to the appearance of field systems and souterrains in the lowlands, and basic questions remain unanswered. For example, did souterrains and large field systems appear at broadly the same time, in a period of stability and cohesion, or sporadically over several centuries?

Some hints may come from the uplands, where analysis of pollen and sediments from lochs and rivers in the Cheviots has produced remarkable evidence of sudden settlement expansion around 250 BC, a pattern repeated over much of northern England and around the Solway Firth. This expansion was not into virgin forest but rather into sparsely populated lands with light forest cover and areas of long-established grazing. But now, quite suddenly, came an episode of massive deforestation and cultivation, doubtless spurred on by the more widespread availability of iron, replacing bronze and stone for axes and ploughshares. Whole

49 The bank and ditch of a linear earthwork are clearly visible as they pass close to the Borders hillfort of Milkieston Rings. The continuation of the earthwork is also visible as it passes through improved pasture.

river catchments were cleared of trees for the cultivation of oats and rye and for grazing. The scale of clearance and cultivation on the formerly wooded slopes was such that tonnes of the newly exposed soil were washed into the Cheviot streams, forming river terraces further down the valleys.

In some areas the hills were carved up by long, linear earthworks, defining boundaries and aiding livestock control (49). The appearance of these 'ranch boundaries' has been linked to a change from the small mixed farming units, such as were dotted around the uplands in earlier centuries, to extensive stock farms.

Such an apparently planned and coordinated assault on the uplands suggests two things: first, the existence of strong, cohesive political structures, for this settlement expansion is unlikely to have been the work of a few intrepid bands of displaced lowland farmers; and, secondly, it suggests that the lowlands were already under intensive exploitation. Indeed, it is tempting to suggest that expansion into the uplands may have followed on quite rapidly from the intensification of agriculture in the lowlands, implying that the latter may have taken place some time around 300 BC.

Woods and wilderness

This picture of a widespread farming settlement, extending even into the southern uplands, bears little resemblance to the impression given by Roman writers, only a few centuries later, of a sprawling forest land. The reason for this discrepancy probably owes more to the classical psyche than to native reality. Roman tales of the vast and vague Caledonian Forest (recently styled the 'myth of Caledon') fit into a wider Mediterranean tradition of tall tales of remote lands where colourful but barbarous inhabitants, fabulous beasts and impenetrable wilderness were all part of the expected package.

The physical evidence of Roman sites in Scotland provides some of the best evidence that the country as a whole was not densely forested. The temporary camps in which the Roman army pitched its tents during repeated military incursions occupied vast acreages of presumably treeless pasture, while the string of Roman signal stations along the Gask Ridge in Perthshire, set up to watch over the movement of native tribes in the AD 80s or 90s, would have made little sense in dense forest. There seems also to have been no shortage of turf, presumably derived from well-established

pasture, to build the superstructure of massive Roman installations like the Antonine Wall.

While locally extensive forests would have remained (such as those from which a Caledonian bear was removed to grace the opening of the Colosseum in Rome), there are signs of stress on the timber supply in the last few centuries BC. Monumental timber houses became rare in the south and east of the country, tending to be replaced by stone-walled structures, sometimes referred to, perhaps unhelpfully, as 'Votadinian houses' after the tribe thought to have occupied Lothian and parts of the Borders. As well as dispensing with timber walling, these houses had relatively small diameters so that they could be roofed with shorter lengths of timber. The wheelhouses that replaced broch towers in parts of the north and west also required minimal amounts of timber for roofing. The burning of coal at Iron Age sites in East Lothian and peat in the Western Isles suggests that surviving stands of timber supplies may have been too precious for use as fuel. Even the Roman army seems to have been forced to use second-rate timber supplies and unsuitable species for major building works.

The parcelling up of the arable lowlands, the expansion into the southern uplands and the unprecedented scale of woodland clearance all point to major social changes in the south and east from around 300 BC. As we saw in chapters 3 and 4, this was also the time at which substantial roundhouses, monuments to local independence and autonomy, were in decline and many hillforts were falling out of use to be replaced by fewer centres and more open settlement. It seems that, as in the broch villages of the north and west, new political structures were emerging among the southern tribes.

6
Identity and power

The romantic notion of the dreaming, boastful, fallible, yet heroic Celt, with its origins in classical description and Victorian mythologizing, still holds a grip on the popular imagination. Yet this stereotypical view of the 'Celtic spirit' allows little room for the social processes reflected in the archaeological record, implying instead a timeless Celtic idyll, antique and unchanging, before its rude exposure to the corrupting influence of intrusive cultural forces.

By contrast, as we have seen, the archaeological picture is full of dynamism and change; in technology, farming practice, land organization and house styles. So do the various written sources have anything to offer the study of the structure and character of Scottish Iron Age societies?

Celtic societies: the documentary basis

Caesar, drawing on his observations in Gaul, described three basic subdivisions of Celtic society in the first century BC: a warrior aristocracy; a learned class of Druids; and the mass of the population. His influential predecessor, Posidonius, a Greek ethnographer writing in the middle of the previous century, had been a little more forthcoming, expanding the learned class to include bards and religious officials called *vates*, and distinguishing military attendants, charioteers, shield-bearers and others among the lower classes. There was probably also an unfree class, although classical authors are unlikely to have found this sufficiently unusual to warrant mention.

Political leadership was not apparently restricted to men. During the first century AD, two women, Cartimandua of the Brigantes in the north of England and Boudicca of the Iceni in the east, were among the most prominent Britons to figure in the classical literature. In Scotland there are no explicit references to women in positions of power, although it has often been claimed that the Picts, who later emerged from the Iron Age tribes in the north east, operated a system of matrilineal inheritance, where kingship and property passed through the female line. If so, it is odd that so few Pictish women appear in the later documentary records and it is, in any case, unlikely that Tacitus would have failed to record such an unclassical practice had it been prevalent in the first century AD.

Beyond suggesting that the Celtic-speaking societies of Britain, Gaul and Ireland in the latter centuries BC were organized in a hierarchical and formal manner, where individuals occupied well-defined social roles, the classical sources are resolutely vague. However, the general model is there and it seems probable that any radically different social structures encountered in Scotland would have been reported. These written sources, however, relate exclusively to the latter part of the Iron Age and describe well-established communities just as they were exposed for the first time to literate and urbanized societies. To explore when and how these tribes formed and their internal institutions crystallized we must turn again to the evidence of archaeology.

Tribal Scotland

By the time of the Roman invasion Scotland was occupied by numerous tribal groups. The Greek geographer Ptolemy, writing in the second century AD, but drawing on earlier accounts, gives a roll-call of the tribes, mostly identified by recognizably Celtic names (**50**). He also provides tantalizingly vague descriptions of their territories: the Selgovae seemingly in the upper Tweed Basin; the Novantae in the south-west; and many more. But Ptolemy's account should not be taken too literally. Problems and omissions could have resulted from Latin misspellings, misunderstandings, copying and mapping errors, any or all of which may have

distorted our view. There is reason to believe, for example, that one of the most important tribes, the Votadini, rather than sprawling from the Forth into the Tweed basin as is usually thought, may have been limited to what is now Lothian, where their post-Roman successors, the Gododdin, were later to be found. Another tribe, the Boresti, is recorded by Tacitus in his account of Agricola's campaigns but fails to appear in Ptolemy's list.

Roman authors refer to similar, though often larger, tribes in Gaul and England, ruled by kings and tribal councils. Tacitus also mentions an exiled Irish king given shelter by Agricola, although he does not refer specifically to any individuals of similar rank in Scotland. Indeed, we know very little of the degree of social organization enjoyed by Ptolemy's tribes. Were they loosely affiliated 'peoples' with some shared ethnicity but little political cohesion, or petty kingdoms with well-established ruling families? The latter is probably more consistent with the written sources: they were able after all to come together in some numbers, however briefly, to confront Agricola. Their appointed leader, a nobleman immortalized by Tacitus as Calgacus, seems to have had a role similar to that of Vercingetorix in Gaul over a century earlier; the temporary military leadership of a tribal confederacy.

Some scholars have pointed to the similarities between Ptolemy's tribal names 'Cornavii', in Caithness, and 'Cornovii', in the west Midlands, and between the 'Damnonii', of the Clyde valley, and the 'Dumnonii', of south-western England, as evidence of close links between tribes occupying Scotland and England during

50 Ptolemy lists numerous tribes in Scotland, most with Celtic names. However, we must be wary of placing too much trust in the precise locations of these groups or in the extent of their territories. Native affairs were by no means Ptolemy's prime concern and there are grounds for believing that he may have greatly simplified the political map in the north, possibly omitting lesser tribes, particularly in the south.

the period of the Roman invasion. While we cannot rule out dynastic links of some form, these similarities could simply have arisen as coincidences based on similar naming principles among Celtic-language speakers, or as scribal errors; unfamiliar northern names being equated incorrectly with those of the rather better-known southern tribes. There is little archaeological evidence to support rather more extreme claims that these similar names reflect mass population movements from south to north at the time of the Roman invasion.

Yet, however problematic our sources may be in detail, there is no reason to doubt the basic impression, gleaned from Ptolemy, of a country occupied by numerous, territorially conscious, tribal groups speaking predominantly, if not entirely, Celtic languages. Given the continuity witnessed in the archaeological record, we can be fairly sure that these tribes had emerged rather earlier than their documented appearance in the second century AD.

Expressions of ethnicity

We might expect the emergence of tribal units to be accompanied by some material expression of tribal or ethnic identity. However, in the early part of our period the surviving artefacts suggest precisely the opposite. During the Later Bronze Age, the status-conscious elites flaunted elaborate bronzes that bore striking similarities to those of their peers elsewhere in Europe. The appeal of these items probably lay as much in their exotic associations as in the time lavished on their production. Indeed, the Bronze Age aristocracy seem to have drawn their status largely from their outside contacts and control of long-distance trade.

From around 700 BC this pattern changed. The collapse of the bronze industry brought an end to long-distance contacts. Communities became rather more inward-looking and status was displayed through communal projects such as fort-building and, at a still more local level, the building of substantial roundhouses. Social position now seems to have been established

through control over land, labour and the agricultural cycle, while the great building schemes helped to set local chiefs at the heart of their communities and stamp their imprint on the land. It was in such communities that kinship and ethnic identity became important concerns.

It has been suggested that the tribal names recorded by Ptolemy imply that some Scottish tribes identified themselves with certain animals; the Epidii (horses) in Kintyre, the Caereni (sheep) and Lugi (ravens) in Sutherland, while the Orcas or Orkney Islands may even derive from 'orci' (young pigs or boars). Interestingly, these names are all found on the northern and western fringes of the country, suggesting that some form of totemic practice may have been a defining part of ethnic identity among the Atlantic Scottish tribes. Animal motifs on north-eastern metalwork of the first centuries BC and AD, such as the boar's head on the Deskford carnyx (see **colour plate 5; 51**) and the stylized snakes on spiral armlets (**52**) may hint at a similar situation there, and similar explanations have been invoked for certain animal symbols inscribed on much later Pictish stones.

The richly decorated pottery found in profusion in the Hebrides, and to a lesser extent in the Northern Isles, seems to have been another medium for ethnic expression (**53**). Potting, like most craft production, was probably carried out by non-specialist farmers and fishers deeply rooted in the traditions of the community, when the demands of food production or procurement allowed. The wheelhouse at Sollas in North Uist yielded around 3000 sherds from a variety of hand-made cooking pots and storage jars, drawing on traditions of form and decoration that do not occur outside the Atlantic zone. While the subtleties encoded within their complex patterns will always elude us, we can at least recognize that these pots expressed to some degree the identity of their makers, perhaps at a variety of scales from household to lineage to tribe.

Most media of ethnic expression, however, were probably rather more transitory in nature

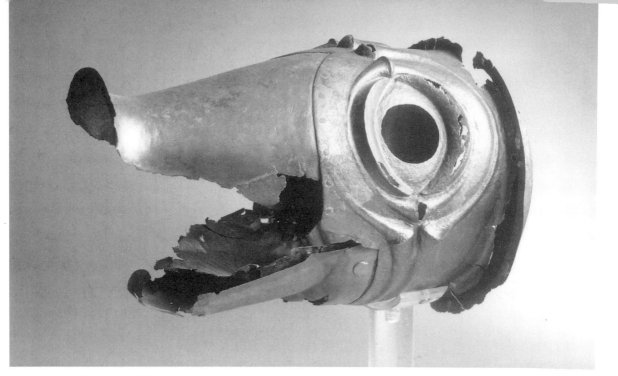

51 This bronze boar's head, found in 1916 in a peat bog near Deskford in Banffshire, formed part of a bronze war-trumpet, or carnyx, probably made in the decades around AD 50. It may even have been used at the battle of Mons Graupius, between the Roman army, under Julius Agricola, and the northern tribes; the battle is generally thought to have taken place somewhere in the north-east.

than pottery or metalwork. Caesar and later Herodian famously record the British custom of painting or tattooing the body with woad, a blue dye, and tattoos can even be discerned on the faces of individuals portrayed on Gaulish coins. Body decoration may well have identified the tribe and status of the wearer. Items associated with weaving, such as spindle whorls, bone combs and loom weights are common finds on settlement sites, suggesting that textiles would have provided another medium for art and symbolism. Ephemeral media such as these may have been the means by which symbols and clan badges were kept alive between their periodic archaeological manifestations in stone or on metalwork.

Cultural boundaries?

The mass of tribal names may mask even deeper divisions. There are strong hints, for example, of a cultural break somewhere between the Firths

52 This snake-headed bronze armlet from Culbin Sands typifies the art styles of the north-east during the early centuries AD. Although the object is distinctively 'Caledonian', the animal head motif is recurrent throughout the Celtic world.

of Forth and Tay. The distinct settlement patterns, with open villages and souterrains to the north and enclosed settlements and forts to the south, have been discussed in previous chapters and presumably reflect differences in the basic organization of society. Artefact types, too, seem often to have been confined either to the north or south of this area (**54**), leading some scholars to postulate a cultural boundary oscillating between the two firths throughout prehistory.

To the Romans the north was distinguished as Caledonia and its inhabitants, according to Tacitus, differed from their southern neighbours by virtue of their 'red hair and massive limbs', while the tribal names associated with the region (the Venicones, Vacomagi and Taezali) are less recognizably Celtic than the rest. Known Caledonians, however, including Calgacus, and a second-century chieftain called Argentocoxos ('silver leg') who negotiated treaties with the Roman emperor Severus, had indisputably Celtic names, and the language of the Pictish kingdom that was later to emerge from the Caledonian tribes was, again, clearly Celtic. The fierce resistance met by the Romans in the north, compared with their apparently smooth passage through southern Scotland, is, however, suggestive of native societies with a rather different outlook.

If one cultural boundary may be dimly discerned between the southern Celts and their Caledonian neighbours, there are hints of another between the Caledonian tribes and those on the Atlantic fringe, where broch villages and dispersed households contrast with the sprawling villages and timber-laced forts of the north-east.

Tribal interaction

In view of the territoriality and social fragmentation that seems to characterize the middle centuries of the first millennium BC, the lack of evidence for inter-tribal contact prior to the Roman incursions comes as little surprise. Steatite, found only in Shetland, was

53 Hebridean Iron Age pottery incorporated a wide range of forms and decorative patterns, giving us some insight into the expressions of regional culture and ethnicity that must originally have existed in a wide range of perishable materials, such as wood, leather, basketry and textiles.

transported to Orkney and to a few sites on the west coast, but apparently not in any significant quantities. Similarly, iron ore must have been traded to some extent, as presumably was timber for the construction of monumental roundhouses in largely treeless areas such as the Northern and Western Isles; but trade in these raw materials is always hard to document.

Better evidence for tribal interaction comes from the occasional appearance of exotic building forms; for example, the 'Wessex-like' ramparts at Burnswark hillfort in Dumfriesshire or the scattered examples of *chevaux-de-frise* (see chapter 4). The movement of high-status individuals, perhaps by marriage or as mercenaries, may be the best explanation for such otherwise mysterious occurrences. Other sporadic finds, such as coral from the fort at Broxmouth, may reflect similar events.

The lack of evidence for routine trading contacts, however, does not reflect a lack of appropriate technologies. Early boats recovered from the Humber estuary suggest that both dug-outs and oak plank vessels, around 15m (50ft) long, would have carried traders, fishermen and warriors around the coasts and along the navigable rivers of the pre-Roman

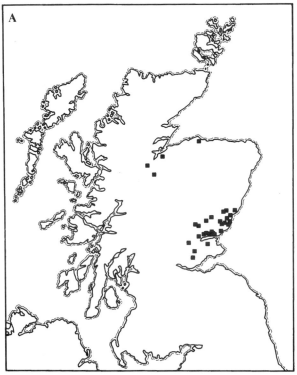

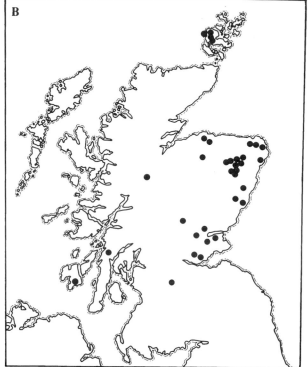

54 A major cultural division seems to have existed at the time of the Roman invasion between northern and southern tribes, with a cultural boundary lying somewhere between the Forth and Tay. The distribution of some artefact and site types seems to have been restricted to the north. A few are shown here: square barrow cemeteries of the early centuries AD; and much earlier decorated carved stone balls, suggesting that this cultural cleavage may have had a lengthy pedigree.

north. Water-borne journeys would have been much swifter and easier than travel over land. Nonetheless, wheeled vehicles had been introduced as early as 1000 BC, as a solid wooden wheel pulled from the Blair Drummond Moss in Stirlingshire testifies, and we know almost nothing of the tracks that might have criss-crossed Scotland before the emplacement of the Roman road network.

Yet, despite sporadic contacts, from around 700–200 BC Scotland appears to have been peopled by self-contained and insular communities. From a background of common languages and conventions, melded in the comparatively cosmopolitan Bronze Age, highly localized traditions and customs would have evolved, dialects would have diverged and cultural differences between communities greatly increased. It is in this context that the tribal groups encountered by the Roman army are perhaps most likely to have emerged.

Expressions of status

By around 100 BC the pattern was changing again and we see a shift from expressions of kinship and ethnicity to expressions of personal status. Perhaps as a northern reflection of an upsurge in trade among the tribes of Gaul and southern England, ultimately spurred on by the establishment of new Mediterranean markets, long-distance contacts were re-established. Scottish manifestations of this renewed activity are limited, however, and many of the goods that probably formed the basis for external trade, such as furs, livestock, textiles and slaves, would leave little or no archaeological trace. However, a pottery model of a bale of fleeces found at Dun Fiadhart in Skye, though probably originating in the Mediterranean, may be a rare reflection of long-distance exchange, and amber beads found at some broch sites also suggest contacts with Scandinavia, outside the conventionally Celtic world. Irish contacts are perhaps most numerous, for example in the distribution of so-called 'door-knob' spear butts from around 200 BC to AD 100 and bone sword pommels of similar date.

This was also the period when communities in Scotland, or at least their leaders, adopted the continental fashions in art and metalwork which have traditionally been used to define Celtic culture. Celtic or La Tène art, with its complex abstract decoration, had originated several centuries earlier in Central Europe. It incorporated a mix of indigenous, Greek and Etruscan motifs including stylized beasts and foliage and rich curvilinear ornament. Although it mostly survives on metalwork, it would doubtless have been applied to numerous perishable materials ranging from timber to textiles to human skin.

The major surviving works of Celtic art reflect the 'heroic', lordly practices of warfare, feasting and drinking. As in the Later Bronze Age, these pieces are rare on domestic sites and were apparently mostly deposited as sacrificial offerings. Among the earliest Scottish finds are the Torrs pony cap and drinking horns found at the base of a Kirkcudbrightshire peat bog (55). The pony cap seems to have been an heirloom, probably made in northern England some time before 100 BC but deposited rather later, having been repaired and brought together with a pair of rather less accomplished drinking horns (see also chapter 7). The Bargrany House scabbard from Ayrshire shows strong affinities with contemporary finds from Ulster and probably also dates to the first century BC (56), while another early hoard, from Shaw Hill in Peeblesshire (see colour plate 11), included three twisted gold torcs buried with around forty Gaulish electrum coins (the only wholly Celtic hoard of coinage yet found in Scotland).

The first century AD saw a huge upsurge in the quantity of prestige objects in circulation, including helmets, torcs and collars, war trumpets, horsegear, swords and scabbards, cauldrons and mirrors (see colour plate 12). One of the finest products of the period was a bronze scabbard found at Mortonhall near Edinburgh some time during the nineteenth century. A strip of metal, decorated with panels of curvilinear ornament, was applied to the front of the scabbard. By using slightly different alloys the makers achieved a clear contrast between the brassy decorative strip and the deep bronze of the scabbard itself, resulting in a remarkable and subtle finish. The Mortonhall scabbard (see colour plate 10) is probably too narrow to have held a fighting sword and may have been made for ritualistic display; perhaps it was hung on a wooden idol, or deposited as a sacrificial offering.

Such fine objects were clearly the work of specialists who must have undergone a lengthy apprenticeship to gain such command over a range of metalworking and decorative techniques. Perhaps their most striking feature is their 'international' quality, with Irish, Gaulish and Roman connections all being manifested, and it is these Celtic or La Tène art styles that show the tribal hierarchies of Scotland most clearly as part of the wider north-west European scene.

Many individual items demonstrate strong links with the tribes of southern Britain, including the East Anglian Iceni and the Brigantes in northern England. The traditional view has been that these were made by displaced Celtic smiths, driven northwards by the Roman occupation. However, as the Torrs pony cap and other early finds demonstrate, Scottish chiefs had re-established contacts with the wider Celtic world as early as the second century BC, well before the advancing Roman army stirred the ethnic soup in the years after AD 43. There is little reason, therefore, to believe that the later finds were not the products of indigenous schools.

The elite connotations of Celtic metalwork must have had their reflections in other aspects of society which are less easy to demonstrate archaeologically. As in the Later Bronze Age,

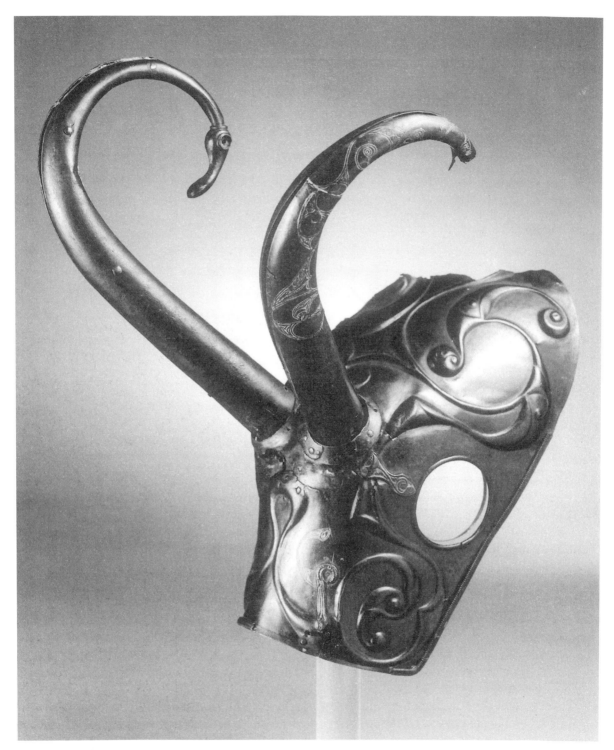

55 The bronze pony cap from Torrs in Kirkcudbrightshire. The two horns were added to the cap in recent times although they probably originated as drinking horns of only slightly later date than the pony cap itself.

the upper classes would presumably have distinguished themselves from those of lower rank through their clothing, speech, demeanour and indulgence in aristocratic pursuits.

Elaborately decorated bronze mirrors, such as one found in 1861 in a bog near Balmaclellan in Kirkcudbrightshire (see **colour plate 12**), suggest an increasing concern with personal appearance. Bone and bronze handles for similar mirrors have been found on south-western crannogs and in the wheelhouse of Bac Mhic Connain in North Uist, while decorated combs and tweezers have been found in other parts of the country.

The ownership of well-bred animals was another way in which chiefs and kings could set themselves apart from their subjects, particularly in a society where ownership of stock would have been a yardstick of wealth. Horses were certainly present throughout much of Scotland, being found in Orkney and the Western Isles as well as further south at sites like Eildon Hill North and Broxmouth. However, their remains on settlement sites are rare compared to the presence of horsegear in hoards and as stray finds. The elaboration of these items and the accounts of chariot warfare in Tacitus suggests that horses were part of the fabric of the elite warrior culture and were prized possessions flaunted in war and in ritual life.

Other animals, such as falcons and hunting dogs, would also have been prized, both as status symbols in their own right and as accessories for hunting. The skull of a North African ape found at the princely seat of Navan fort, in Ulster, suggests that even more exotic animals might have graced the courts of northern nobles in the closing centuries BC.

While we can recognize a new cosmopolitan tendency in these elites, lordly fashions during the early centuries AD seem to have perpetuated the ancient divide between the tribes north and south of the Forth–Clyde line. Certain bronze objects, notably massive armlets and spiral bracelets in the form of snakes (see **52**), are overwhelmingly northern in their distribution (see **54**). Interestingly, these finds do not extend greatly into the far north and the islands, reinforcing the earlier suggestion of a further cultural divide between Atlantic Scotland and the north-east.

Three ages?

Taking a broader view of these changes in the nature of tribal society, we can begin to discern three periods of development, although the boundaries between them remain muddy and hard to date. In the first period, from around 1000 BC to 700 BC, the social elite drew their authority from their control over the production and distribution of bronze and other goods, and expressed their status by the ostentatious sacrifice of exotic and costly weaponry. Theirs was an warrior ideology based on martial

56 The Bargany House scabbard from Ayrshire. Part of the original sword blade is still contained within the scabbard. The sword and scabbard were deliberately bent before being deposited.

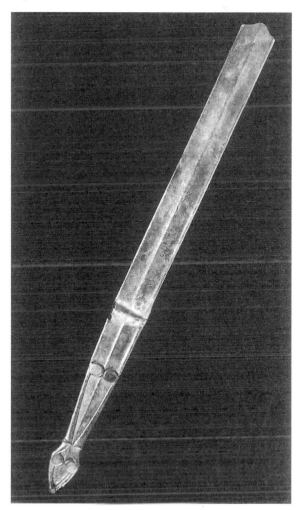

symbolism and outside contacts, with little overt sign of regional or tribal identities.

From around 700 BC to perhaps 200 BC, there was still a warrior elite, at least in southern Scotland, but one which drew its power from control over the people, the land and agricultural production. There was an apparent multiplicity of petty chiefs whose essentially local power was expressed through community works, such as hillforts and enclosed settlements of all shapes and sizes. In many areas individual land-holding families had a large degree of independence, expressed in the elaborate homesteads, crannogs and Atlantic roundhouses. It was in this period of social fragmentation that the tribal identities were probably forged. However, there seems to have been some gradual centralization of power, and by around 300 BC some tribes were sufficiently well organized to embark on great collective projects: the establishment of landscape boundaries, land improvements and the deforestation of the uplands for agriculture.

The third period, from perhaps 200 BC until the AD 80s, saw a further radical change. It is in this period that we see the emergence of societies which we can begin to compare with the Celtic stereotype; these people mostly spoke Celtic languages and had adopted Celtic art styles of continental origin. Their leaders again adhered to a warrior ideology, and supported specialist craftsmen trained in a cosmopolitan style. This Celtic cultural milieu seems to reflect a period of powerful leadership and relatively stable social conditions; the latter reflected by undefended settlements in the south and east and tightly knit broch villages in the far north. An open settlement at New Mains in East Lothian, which has yielded a bronze spiral armlet and ring, and a bronze torc or neck decoration, along with a mix of Roman and native pottery, suggests the type of high-status undefended settlement which appears to have replaced the multiplicity of earlier hillforts in the south. Yet society had not come full circle. Evidence remained of tribalism and deep cultural divisions; warfare, feuding and raiding were probably still rife, particularly around the fringes of tribal territories.

By the turn of the millennium these long centuries of development were already coming to an end. The Roman army under Caesar had already campaigned, albeit inconclusively, in the south of England, and we can assume that the Scottish tribes were aware of these distant clashes. But before we turn to the Roman encounter with Scotland it remains to explore the religious beliefs and practices that underpinned the indigenous Celtic tribes.

7
Death and belief

Lost beliefs

Modern western societies are a poor model for understanding prehistoric religion. For most of us, religion is a clearly demarcated part of life. But in many non-western societies it is, as the ethnologist William Goode said, 'not something which is only believed: it is lived'. For the Iron Age Celts, religion, ritual and superstition would have permeated all aspects of life, from building a house or ploughing a field to making a journey or exchanging gifts.

Like many farming peoples, for thousands of years the ancestors of the Celts had lived their lives according to the seasons and calculated time by the movement of the sun, moon and stars. Most of the ritual acts discussed in this chapter probably marked important points in the agricultural cycle. The importance of the moon is demonstrated by a bronze calendar dating to the first century BC, from Coligny in what was Celtic Gaul, inscribed with sixty-two lunar months, and marking Beltane (now May Day) and other festivals based on the farming year.

Most of our knowledge of Celtic religion derives from the classical and Irish texts, embellished by a less coherent, but nonetheless weighty, body of archaeological data and contemporary inscriptions. The range of the literary descriptions is narrow: on the one hand we have a snapshot of Gaul and southern England as the indigenous cultures were subsumed within the Roman Empire, although some later inscriptions help to fill out the

record; on the other a distant echo of pagan Irish beliefs chopped and changed by Christian monks. Given the likely diversity of Celtic beliefs and practices, it is easy to question the relevance of these texts to people in Scotland whose religious lives attracted no comment. But these documents provide at least a starting-point from which to discuss the diverse archaeological evidence for Celtic religion in Scotland.

The gods

One count of inscriptions and dedications attested to some 400 Celtic gods worshipped in the Roman period alone. Some would have been local deities, linked to rivers, lakes and mountains, while others had a wider currency and were associated with universal functions or attributes, much in the manner of modern saints. The Romans, with their own heterogeneous pantheon, were quick to tidy up Celtic beliefs, equating native deities with their classical equivalents. Mars, for example, came to be identified with at least sixty-nine Celtic gods.

Only a few likely representations of Celtic gods have been found in Scotland. In 1880, workmen digging foundations for a wall at Ballachulish came upon an almost life-sized female figure crudely carved in oak with inset eyes of quartz (57). It lay face down on gravel under more than 3m (10ft) of peat, below a collapsed wicker structure, where it had been placed, according to radiocarbon dating, around 700–500 BC (58). The sharp outlines of the

57 The Ballachulish figure shortly after its discovery in 1880. The arms, hands and fingers are carved into the trunk.

carving, when first found, show that it did not lie for long on the surface but must have been buried deliberately in the peat or dumped in a stagnant pool. Perhaps a timber shrine had been deliberately cast down or maybe the disposal of the figure mimicked the ritual of drowning criminals under a wooden hurdle; a punishment attested in the literary sources and perhaps illustrated by some of the Danish bog bodies.

Another deity is probably represented by a granite tricephalos (a three-headed figure), with a stereotypically Celtic drooping moustache, dating to between 200 BC and AD 100. This carving, the size of a small football, was found in Sutherland in the early years of this century. It was made of a non-Scottish stone and may have been brought from Gaul. How it came to be in the north of Scotland is unknown, but it seems to hint at a degree of religious contact between Scotland and Gaul prior to the Roman invasion.

The Druids

Even closer religious links are implied by the classical and Irish writers who are unanimous in ascribing to the Celts a class of religious specialists known as Druids. Caesar describes this shadowy priesthood as a powerful and hierarchical, pan-tribal organization. Adherents all over Gaul and Britain, where the cult apparently originated, underwent a rigorous twenty-year training to memorize their unwritten and arcane knowledge. They met, Caesar claims, at fixed times, presumably the key Celtic festivals, at a sacred centre overseen by a chief Druid. As well as their priestly function, Caesar's Druids doubled as teachers, judges and doctors and occupied an esteemed position in the hierarchies of their tribes.

Like later Christian priests, Druids seem to have played a key role in secular life, lending divine endorsement to the Celtic aristocracy.

The Irish records, although rather later in date, chronicle their crucial role in supporting kings whose right to their earthly position was established through appeal to the gods. Briochan, the magician priest ousted by St Columba from the court of the Pictish king Brude in the sixth century AD, may have been one of the last individuals to command such a role in Scotland.

Although Caesar may have exaggerated their cohesion and influence (and indeed, may have conflated roles held quite distinct by the Celts into the Druid repertoire) it appears that the Druids were a well organized and influential

58 The Ballachulish figure originally seems to have stood in a wicker or wattle structure, seen here in an artist's reconstruction.

group, at least in the first century BC. The existence of a formal priesthood presupposes a common pantheon and a shared set of beliefs sufficiently baroque to require the attention of dedicated specialists.

However, for Iron Age Scotland, the written records are unhelpful and archaeology can scarcely be expected to deliver us incontrovertible Druids. All that we can say is that if the peoples living in Scotland had religious beliefs distinct from other Celts, and priests who were not Druids, then the Romans failed to report it.

Places of worship

The classical records suggest that Celtic religion was practised in natural places, such as groves, forest clearings, pools, lakes and islands, rather than in the monumental buildings familiar to the Romans and Greeks, so it is unsurprising that overtly ritual sites are hard to find.

Most favoured for communion with the supernatural world were liminal places, such as hills between earth and sky, caves between the living world and the underworld, settlement boundaries between the domestic and the wild, and rivers between land and sea. Certain islands, too, seem to have been regarded as sacred. Anglesey, according to Tacitus, was a Druid preserve at the time of the Roman invasion, while Plutarch relates the story of a traveller, Demetrius of Tarsus, who had visited other holy islands (possibly in the Hebrides), during Agricola's campaigns. The attraction of remote islands for the later Celtic Christian monks may even reflect this much earlier tradition.

Watery places

Bogs, rivers and lakes are our most plentiful source of bronzes from the earlier part of the first millennium BC well into the Roman period. While there is, as yet, no known Scottish equivalent of the artificial pool near Navan fort in Ulster, where animal and human offerings were placed amid swords, pottery and clay moulds from around 900 BC, there are hints that similar sites may exist. Many hillforts, such as Barry Hill in Perthshire and Finavon in Angus, enclose large wells or cisterns that may have been used for more than simple utilitarian purposes. Northern broch towers, like Midhowe in Orkney and Crosskirk in Caithness, often contained elaborate wells reached by steps carved from the rock. Even in the historical Pictish period, the great promontory fort at Burghead in Moray had a well-built vaulted

chamber containing a well that might have acted as a place of ritual and sacrifice rather than as a simple water source.

Temples and sanctuaries

In both Gaul and England the immediately pre-Roman period saw the emergence of rather more formal temples, presumably influenced by Mediterranean fashions. In Scotland, however, where Roman influence was much less strong, there is little evidence yet for unambiguously religious buildings at this date.

There is some evidence nonetheless for the re-use of much older religious monuments. A list of place-names in Roman Britain, probably copied from an earlier map at Ravenna in the sixth century AD, includes *Medio Nemeton* ('middle sanctuary'), somewhere close to the Antonine Wall. Stuart Piggott has suggested that this might refer to the Neolithic henge monument on Cairnpapple Hill in West Lothian, where there is a scatter of late burials possibly dating to the Roman period (59). The site commands views as far east as the Bass Rock, north to Schiehallion in Perthshire and west to Arran, so could certainly justify the name. Indeed knowing what little we do of Celtic religion it is hard to

59 Cairnpapple, West Lothian: was this ritual enclosure or 'henge', originating around 3000 BC, the *Medio Nemeton* or 'middle sanctuary' of the Scottish Celts mentioned by the Romans? The pits shown in the foreground of this view are probably Iron Age graves.

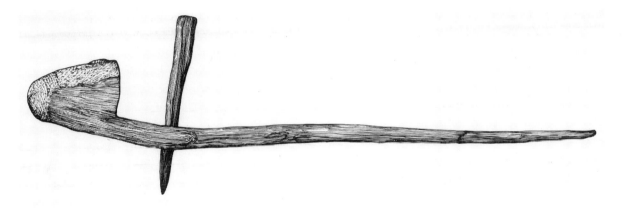

60 Sometime in the early centuries AD this wooden ard, or early ploughing implement, was placed in the ditch of the probably earlier 'henge' monument at Pict's Knowe in south-west Scotland.

imagine that a site with ritual associations in such a dramatic location would have been ignored in the Iron Age.

Another ancient ritual site apparently still venerated was Pict's Knowe, a small henge monument in south-west Scotland. A simple wooden ard had been placed in the ditch directly opposite the entrance, probably in the second or third centuries AD (60). Many other monuments of the Neolithic and Bronze Ages may also have had lengthy Celtic after lives, although little material evidence may have accumulated to prove it.

Caves
At the end of the last century, a number of burials, both male and female, were found in the MacArthur Cave, near Oban in Argyll. These were originally thought to date to a period thousands of years before the Iron Age, because of the presence in the cave of Mesolithic bone tools, but radiocarbon dating has now placed them in the middle of the first millennium BC. Similar burials from other caves and rock shelters around Oban may well belong to the same burial tradition, and the presence of children as well as adults of both sexes suggests that these caves may have been used as cemeteries by small communities in the vicinity.

Other Scottish caves witnessed rather more complex ritual activity. The Sculptor's Cave is a deep natural cleft cut into a sandstone coastal cliff near Covesea on the Moray Firth. This dark recess was used for ritual purposes over many centuries, though perhaps intermittently, from around 800 BC through to the sixth or seventh centuries AD when a series of Pictish symbols was carved around the entrance. A series of carved crosses, including one from the twelfth century AD, shows that even in medieval Christian times the site retained some religious resonance. When Sylvia Benton visited the cave in 1928, prior to her excavations, she observed that the floor even then was 'strewn with human bones'.

The Sculptor's Cave appears to have served originally as an ossuary, probably in the Later Bronze Age. Records of the early excavations are rather sketchy but refer to some 2000 human bones, including a large proportion of children, and numerous bronze artefacts. Many of the dead had been beheaded. While later activity may have been more sporadic, and there is no sign of habitation in the early centuries AD, valuable and exotic objects including fake Roman coins, bronze tweezers and pins were deposited, perhaps as offerings to underworld deities.

Elsewhere, early records offer tantalizing hints of sacrificial burial. A cave at Seacliff in East Lothian contained the bones of two newborn infants along with fragments of Iron Age pottery below a huge stone, possibly an altar. Although vague, such records suggest that Sculptor's Cave may not have been unique.

Rites of sacrifice

Classical accounts of Celtic religion dwell on acts of sacrifice. The offering of material wealth to the gods, in return for favours, to ensure good luck or as simple bribes, is common in accounts of the Celts, and far from alien to classical societies of the same period. Mounds of valuable possessions, booty and trophies of war, were apparently heaped in sacred places, enclosures and pools, inviolable on pain of death. This wealth could comprise elaborate jewellery or weaponry, but on occasion could be altogether more grisly.

Offerings of wealth

The great majority of bronze weapons and tools from the early centuries of the first millennium BC were either recovered as isolated finds or formed part of metalwork hoards (**61**). Although functional interpretations are often put forward to explain these hoards (explaining them away as tinker's caches, or personal property hastily buried in times of danger), their position in lakes, pools and bogs, where recovery was unlikely, suggests that most were votive offerings to pagan deities.

One such hoard, from a peat bog at Adabrock, near the northern tip of Lewis, comprised tools such as gouges, a hammer, socketed axe, chisel and whetstones, along with a spearhead, beads of amber, gold and glass, and fragments of a sheet bronze vessel. Another, dredged from Duddingston Loch in Edinburgh in 1778, comprised a mass of swords and spearheads along with human and animal bones.

The practice of depositing bronzes seems to have died out in Scotland by around 500 BC, by which time bronze itself was in sharp decline as a material for weapon and tool manufacture. However, it may be that many later iron objects

61 Part of a hoard of Later Bronze Age metalwork recovered from Duddingston Loch, Edinburgh.

and perishable offerings continued to be deposited but have simply not survived.

A few centuries later hoards reappear in the archaeological record, this time displaying marked regional variation. A recent study has characterized most hoards north of the Forth as fairly small, comprising perhaps a handful of personal ornaments in the local tradition, for example, massive armlets. To the south they were more varied and often much larger; horse fittings and vessels accompanied jewellery, and the hoards often included Roman goods. A few southern hoards, like the one from Carlingwark Loch in Kirkcudbrightshire, contained large bronze cauldrons and other iron objects. Unlike the hoards of earlier centuries, however, weapons were noticeably rare.

This apparent boundary coincides with that observed in the previous chapter as marking a possible line of cultural cleavage in Scotland between the southern tribes and the 'Caledonian' tribes to the north of the Forth or Tay.

Human sacrifice

The long-lived tradition of sacrifice may not have been restricted to material possessions. Several classical writers alleged that the Gauls burnt prisoners in wicker cages, and Tacitus chronicles the sacrifice of prisoners by Druid

62 Human sacrifice: a ritual drowning at the hands of a grim Celtic deity depicted on the Gundestrup cauldron from Denmark.

priests in Anglesey during the Roman campaigns of AD 60, adding that the entrails of these unfortunates were sometimes used to prophesy future events. The poet Lucan gave an especially vivid account of ritual slaughter by the Gauls in the presence of rude idols, in gory forest sanctuaries 'where birds feared to perch'.

While some of these accounts may simply peddle Roman propaganda, or pander to Mediterranean expectations of Celtic barbarity, there is a small and ambiguous body of archaeological evidence to back them up. The most graphic is the ritual drowning depicted on the Gundestrup cauldron from Denmark, where a horned god is shown bundling his victim into a large vessel or well (62). Yet the credentials of this oft-quoted illustration of Celtic religious practice are somewhat undermined by an eclectic symbolism that mixes conventionally Celtic motifs, like the horned god, the cauldron and the boar-headed war trumpet, with Indian elephants. That the cauldron was found and almost certainly produced outside the traditional Celtic regions underlines further the dangers of defining a uniquely Celtic religious tradition.

Other hints can be found within the British Isles. A corpse dumped in a bog at Lindow in Cheshire in the last centuries BC, for example, was that of a man who had been struck on the head, strangled and had his throat cut: not an opportunistic murder and unlikely to have been accidental. Elsewhere, in southern England, human burials have been found in pits directly below the ramparts of such forts as Maiden Castle, Hod Hill and South Cadbury, illustrating the use of the dead as foundation offerings. Also in the south, disused grain pits at Danebury hillfort in Hampshire contained fragments of human corpses, deliberately butchered and selectively deposited. Perhaps these are remnants of human offerings to an underworld god, as payment for a good harvest or successful raid.

Totemism and animal offerings
The ritual slaughter of animals unsurprisingly attracted little comment from classical writers, although it was undoubtedly as regular an occurrence throughout the Celtic world as it was around the Mediterranean. Actual archaeological evidence for ritualized animal sacrifice can be hard to differentiate from normal butchery, particularly if the animal was consumed as part of the religious observance. Some votive deposits, however, do give a fairly clear illustration of animal sacrifice in operation, for example, the burial of a horse under one of the ramparts on Eildon Hill North, and a butchered ewe in a pit below a rampart at Broxmouth; the wheelhouses of the Atlantic north-west contain many more (see below).

Skulls of cattle, sheep, horse and pigs placed, along with human cremations, in the disused souterrains at Dalladies, Kincardineshire, like the sacrificial deposits of animals and sometimes human body parts in grain storage pits in southern England, seem to betray the intimate links between religion and the agricultural cycle. Some animals, however, may have been venerated during the Iron Age, particularly those like the horse or boar that may have been adopted as clan badges by certain tribes, or deer which appear as a motif on Hebridean pottery (see chapter 6). It has even been suggested that the Torrs pony cap (see **55**), which would have been awkward and ill-fitting, may have formed part of a mask for a 'pantomime horse' as seen performing in some religious ceremony or festival on the broadly contemporary bronze bucket from Aylesford in Kent. The horns found with the pony cap may have been affixed some time after its original manufacture to add a further fantastical dimension to the performance: horned horses are represented on the Gundestrup cauldron and on Iron Age fire-dogs from Wales.

The cult of the head

Numerous references, from Polybius writing of the Battle of Telamon in 225 BC to the later Christian Irish authors, attest to the Celtic predilection for collecting the severed heads of their enemies. Posidonius further related how the Gauls nailed the heads of vanquished enemies to their houses and preserved others in cedar oil for permanent display. While some Roman writers probably played up the head-hunting aspect of Celtic warfare for propaganda purposes, there is a scatter of supporting evidence from across Celtic Europe. Monumental stone structures with niches cut to hold human skulls at Entremont in southern France (the 'Hall of Skulls') were apparently desecrated by the Roman army in 123 BC, while skulls punctured by iron nails were found at Puig Castellar in Spain. Human heads and weaponry were placed in the waters of the Thames even during the Roman period and human skulls were among the votive deposits in Coventina's Well on Hadrian's Wall.

In Scotland, we have already seen the evidence for the beheading of children and adults in Sculptor's Cave, but there are numerous other examples of special attention being paid to the human head. One of the most intriguing aspects of the communal cist burial at Lochend in East Lothian (see below) was the puzzle of the missing heads. Not only were at least seven skulls absent from the cist but a further six were apparently found in the loose earth at the opening, perhaps placed there for display. Neck vertebrae within the cist showed damage consistent with (in the evocative words of the bone analyst) 'a deep sword cut to the neck at the time of death'. A severed head has also recently been found in the post-broch occupation levels at Scatness in Shetland.

As late as the ninth century AD, at the end of the Pictish period, Sueno's Stone, the great Moray cross slab, depicts a battle scene of quite extraordinary violence (63). It is tempting to see the echoes of Celtic head-hunting in its graphic portrayal of the decapitation of prisoners of war. Stone carved heads, such as the one reputed to have been found dumped in the well

63 Sueno's stone, Moray: does this detail, showing, on the left, a row of decapitated prisoners, from the elaborate battle scene on the 9th-century AD Pictish stone echo the earlier Celtic cult of the head?

in the fort at Burghead, may represent a milder aspect of this gory practice.

In many societies where warfare is endemic the removal of heads can symbolize the completeness of the enemies' subjugation rather than the simple collection of gory battle trophies. Ritualized cannibalism takes this a stage further. Mentions of cannibalism are made in the Irish Celtic sources, while Roman writers attest that the Celts might resort to cannibalism in times of extreme food shortage, such as sieges. But the evidence for institutionalized, even religious cannibalism, is perhaps more interesting. Fragmentary skulls found in the fort at Broxmouth, in numbers disproportionate to other human remains, show frequent signs of butchery consistent with either scalping or the removal of brains for consumption. 'Waste' fragments from this process occurred in the fort rather than outside, suggesting that cannibalism is the more likely option, since scalping presumably would have taken place on the battlefield. The lack of such disfigurement among the cemetery population at Broxmouth suggests that cannibalism was restricted to particular individuals, perhaps outsiders or enemies.

While the jury must remain out on the question of a long-lived and widespread cult of the human head in Scotland, the evidence from sites like Sculptor's Cave and Lochend provides some important circumstantial evidence.

Burial

Despite the regular occurrence of stray fragments of human bone on settlements, formal Iron Age burials are notoriously rare in Britain prior to the first century AD, although the same cannot be said for much of Europe. By the end of the Bronze Age cremation was the dominant burial rite throughout Britain, the ashes often being placed in pots, pits or cairns. Around 700 BC, however, cremations more or less disappear from the archaeological record.

Some indications are now appearing, however, to suggest that some simple burials and small cemeteries may date to the first millennium

BC. Just outside the fort at Broxmouth in East Lothian, for example, lay nine rough oval grave pits, some lined with stones. The dead were placed on their sides, crouched or with their legs lightly flexed, and seem to have been buried during the last three centuries BC. Similar graves from the nearby palisaded enclosure of Dryburn Bridge may date from two or three centuries earlier. The Argyll cave burials, mentioned earlier, may represent another local variant in this tradition of small community cemeteries. Before the advent of radiocarbon dating, such small cemeteries lacking grave goods could not have been ascribed to any particular period, so many more may have gone unrecognized.

This tradition of small community burials fits in well with the wider picture of society during the middle centuries of the millennium. This, after all, was the period of social fragmentation, when communities kept to themselves and when so much labour was spent on building forts, enclosures and other, essentially communal projects.

These cemeteries, however, cannot account for all Iron Age deaths. Burial at sea, or in rivers, might accord with the Celtic veneration of watery places and would leave little or no physical trace. Similarly, cremation might have simply continued to be practised, but the ashes scattered rather than buried (although we might expect to find some evidence of funeral pyres).

Another possibility favoured by many archaeologists is excarnation, where the dead are exposed (for example on scaffolds or trees, or in enclosures or caves) until the flesh has rotted from the bones. Such rites, aimed at freeing the spirit from the body, were practised until quite recently by native Americans and can be discerned among the first farming groups in Scotland. However, no obvious Iron Age excarnation sites have been found and many burials manifestly have not been subject to exposure. Indeed, if this rite had persisted into the Roman period it is likely that Caesar and others would have highlighted it as a further example of Celtic barbarity.

Cist burials of the early centuries AD

A great many more burials can be ascribed to the first and second centuries AD, most comprising inhumations, or very occasionally cremations, in cists. These were essentially stone boxes lining pits or occasionally built into cairns, reviving a mode of burial common in the Early Bronze Age.

By far the most unusual of these burials was found at Lochend in East Lothian, where a large stone cist was found, containing the bones of at least twenty adults and a child. The under-representation of children contrasts with the situation in the rather earlier Sculptor's Cave and the Oban cave cemeteries and reflects a new selectivity about which members of the community were entitled to particular modes of burial. The bodies had been put into the cist one by one over many years. On each occasion one of the slabs was raised, the new burial was inserted and covered with a thin layer of earth and stones. Earlier burials were pushed back into the corners, creating a mass of jumbled bones. Right from the start this seems to have been intended as a burial 'vault' (rather than a single grave which simply grew and grew), since the first burial, a woman in her forties, had been tucked into a fairly small part of the cist floor.

Most of the Lochend bodies had been buried without obvious grave goods, but two iron pins and a red enamel stud found within the grave suggest that some of the burials took place in the first or second centuries AD. The communal nature of the burial rite, and the mixing up of the bones, comes as something of a surprise for this period, recalling as it does the burial practices of the earliest farming communities in Scotland, around 3000 years earlier (see Patrick Ashmore's *Neolithic and Bronze Age Scotland* in this series).

Elsewhere, multiple cist burials are very rare. At Moredun in Midlothian two adults were buried together in a short cist along with jewellery dated to around the second century AD (**64**), while a cairn at Ackergill in Caithness contained at least four individuals, one wearing a chain of likely first- or second-century AD date. The closest parallel for Lochend, however, was found almost 50 miles south on the Northumbrian coast at Beadnell, where another cist tomb was found to contain the bones of around eighteen people.

Many simpler cist burials date to the same general period as Lochend. A recently excavated inhumation from Galson in Lewis was accompanied by a small vessel with incised decoration, similar to material from wheelhouses of the first centuries BC and AD. Another, found some years ago during the construction of Stornoway airport, was accompanied by three pots, a weaving comb and spindle whorl. At Camelon, beside a Roman fort just north of the Antonine Wall, a crude stone cist contained the remains of a man buried with an iron sword. The sword was probably a Roman infantry *gladius*, although the owner may well have been a Celt. Two further corpses from the same area were found buried with two spears, a sword and the remains of a shield.

Perhaps even more intriguing than these warrior burials was a long cist at Burnmouth, in Berwickshire, which contained an adult laid out on his right side with a joint of pork, an iron knife and two bronze spoons (**65**). These spoons

64 A cist burial under excavation at Moredun, Edinburgh, in 1903.

were of a distinctive form similar to pairs from France, Ireland and England, and seem to date to AD 50–100. In every case, one of the spoons is perforated while the other is incised with a cross, and the handles bear curvilinear Celtic decoration. The virtually identical design of these items, in the absence of any functional explanation, seems to argue for a shared religious symbolism and perhaps similar religious rites across a wide area. Perhaps the dead man at Burnmouth was involved in the ritual life of his community; perhaps he was even a Druid.

Barrow cemeteries

Most of the cists described above have been found singly and with no indication of above-ground markers, covering mounds or barrows. However, in recent years numerous barrow cemeteries have been discovered in eastern

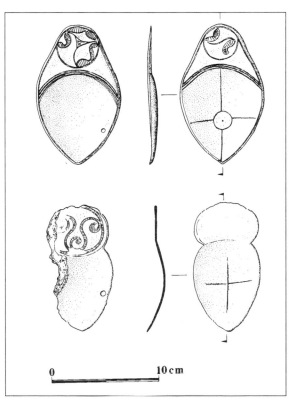

65 Two pairs of bronze 'spoons', from a grave at Burnmouth, Berwickshire (top) and from Westmorland in England (bottom). The distinctive patterning is replicated exactly on several other pairs from Ireland, England and France.

97

66 A square and round barrow cemetery at Rossie, near Abernyte.

Scotland, north of the Forth. The ditches of round and square barrows are visible from the air as cropmarks, often in small clustered cemeteries (66). Square barrow cemeteries dating to the Iron Age have long been known in eastern Yorkshire and in north-east France. In both areas the dead were buried with their prized possessions, occasionally including dismantled chariots. More recently, barrows of similar appearance have been found as far afield as Slovakia and Hungary.

At Boysack Mills in Angus one square barrow was found to have covered a deep central grave pit. At the base lay a wooden coffin containing a skeleton, laid out flat with an iron pin that had formerly held its clothing in place. Although this pin dates to the first or second centuries AD, detailed comparisons with upstanding square and rectangular cairns, found mostly in northern Scotland, suggest that the use of these cemeteries may extend well into the post-Roman period.

Domestic rituals in the north

A curious series of deposits recovered from wheelhouses in the Western Isles shed some light on an aspect of Iron Age ritual that escapes note in the literary sources. At Sollas in North Uist, around 150 pits had been dug into the soft sand floor of the wheelhouse (67). Of these, around 60 contained animal bone while the rest may well have held other perishable materials, such as plant foods. Most of the ritual deposits at Sollas

came from small, often inter-cutting, pits dug during the life of the building. These contained a bewildering menagerie of mutilated creatures. Three held entire sheep, dismembered to fit. Others were stuffed with generous chunks of cattle and one unfortunate pig was also present. Burnt or cremated animal bone was also plentiful, sometimes in pottery vessels. However, not all the pits held animal bone: in one tiny pit was a bronze-working crucible covered with carefully placed mica plates. Over another was the upper stone of a rotary quern. It has been suggested that its central hole may have enabled the pouring of libations into the pit or perhaps formed a conduit for communication with the spirits of the underworld.

The cell directly opposite the wheelhouse entrance seems to have attracted the greatest concentration of these offerings, suggesting that it held some special status. Similarly at A' Cheardach Mhor, a South Uist wheelhouse, the equivalent cell contained a peculiar deposit of sheep long bones thrust vertically into its floor. At Cnip, in Lewis, votive deposits had been placed behind the walls as they were built, among them the head of a great auk and a complete pottery vessel (original contents unknown).

Humans were not exempt from these rituals. At Hornish Point in South Uist, the floor of a radially partitioned structure, similar in some ways to the wheelhouses, held four pits containing the quartered body of a young boy of about twelve years of age, and the remains of young sheep and cattle. The butchering of this youth, a spina bifida sufferer, had clearly happened some time after his death, since his body had partially decomposed before being cut up. We cannot now tell whether this was a deliberate human sacrifice or whether his death was simply coincidental with the erection of the new building.

Other human remains have been found on wheelhouse sites. At Cnip the top of a human skull was laid, together with pottery fragments, in a hollow scooped from the sand in an abandoned wheelhouse. Another skull fragment had been shaved with a knife and dumped in a midden, while yet another had been drilled with an 'hourglass' perforation. While the latter might evoke Posidonius' dramatic images of severed heads hanging in the house as trophies, it appears that, in this case, the skull was not fresh, and the piece may have been picked up as a stray fragment.

These deposits imply a highly ritualized approach to domestic life which belies the superficial impression of wheelhouses as simple farming settlements familiar from peasant cultures of the not-so-ancient past. Houses seem to have been insulated and protected from the outer 'wild' world by the placing of these ritually charged deposits at key boundary points: in their walls and floors, and at entrances. Perhaps similar thought processes lay behind the placing of already ancient cup-marked stones in the walls of souterrains, as at Pitcur in Angus, or the incorporation of rotary

querns into the walls and floors of both northern and southern roundhouses.

Whether the deposition of animal offerings, so important in the Hebrides in the first centuries BC and AD, was widespread across the rest of Scotland is likely to remain unknown, since deposits like those at Sollas and Cnip would simply not survive in most plough-damaged settlements in the lowlands. However, the general lack of formal burial and ritual sites in the heyday of monumental roundhouse building does suggest that the house may have been the main forum for the sacred as well as profane aspects of community life, of which sacrifice may have been a central part.

Roundhouse cosmology

Ritual aspects of Iron Age houses are not restricted to special or votive deposits. Right across Britain, for example, patterns can be detected in the orientation of roundhouse entrances; the majority being set towards the east or south-east, perhaps to face the rising sun (particularly at equinox and mid-winter solstice) which may have been identified with birth and renewal. It has been suggested that, as in some societies today, the prevailing cosmology or world view determined the proper way to lay out houses and settlement compounds. West-facing structures, set towards the setting sun, may have been associated with death and barrenness or, in the case of some broch towers, as an indication of high status and dominance over nature.

Such beliefs would certainly not be out of keeping with the practices seen to such dramatic effect in the Hebridean wheelhouses. The formal radial and cellular patterning which seems to have been a recurrent feature across otherwise distinct architectural traditions, such as broch towers, wheelhouses and ring-ditch houses, similarly suggests that well-established codes governed the lay-out of the house.

The existence of such complex and long-lived patterns of belief challenges any concept of a Europe-wide Celtic religion, since houses in continental Europe were invariably rectangular

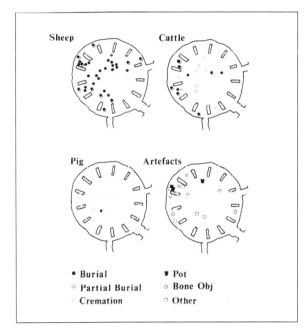

67 The floor of the wheelhouse at Sollas contained a mass of pits filled with votive offerings. Some were probably foundation deposits, dug when the house was built while others, particularly those containing sheep, cattle and pigs, were placed in small pits under the sand floor while the building was occupied and may have marked particular events or projects in the life of the community.

and quite unrelated to the British roundhouses. Indeed, roundhouses in Scotland long pre-date the cosmopolitan cultural milieu of the Later Bronze Age, and may reflect a much earlier stratum of religious thinking that survived in some places, in broadly recognizable form, as late as the Roman period.

Celtic religion in Scotland

Archaeology can give only a fragmentary reflection of prehistoric religious life. The exceptional survival of the wooden idol from Ballachulish serves to show how much Iron Age religious symbolism was invested in long-vanished perishable materials, while the later Irish texts provide a flavour of the myths, songs, stories and legends that we have lost. Yet archaeology can provide a broad outline of changing religious practice; at least enough to begin to relate religion to other aspects of Iron Age society. For example, there was clearly never any one definable 'Celtic religion'; a timeless, unchanging system of beliefs. The rites practised in the Sculptor's Cave around 800 BC would probably have been unintelligible to one of Caesar's Druids. Nonetheless, common themes, like the veneration of the head and relative lack of formal burials, seem to have been long-lived and transcended tribal boundaries.

Not surprisingly, ritual and religious life reflects wider changes in society, and the threefold division of social change described in chapter 6 can be discerned to some degree amid the patchwork of burials, hoards and household rituals.

The dominance of martial symbols in Later Bronze Age hoards suggests that ritual life was thoroughly imbued with the values of a warrior aristocracy. The disappearance of these hoards occurred broadly in parallel with the emergence of hillforts and enclosed settlements, and for several centuries the only real intimation of ritual life was to be the presence of small community cemeteries. Much of the skill and surplus labour formerly expended on producing and obtaining bronzes for display and ritualized destruction seems to have been transferred to the building and maintenance of elaborate but communal defences; again, perhaps bolstering a warrior ideology but one identified with the locality and the tribe, drawing its authority from kinship rather than from divine sanction or exotic connections.

The re-emergence of powerful chiefs or kings can be traced from around the first century BC when ritual life again becomes much more visible in the archaeological record. Complex and varied burials, often with grave goods, suggest a fairly well-formed belief in the after-life, and their appearance ties in closely with the upsurge in prestige metalwork and the adoption of Celtic art styles in Scotland. Signs of vocation or social status in burials, like the Camelon swords or the Burnmouth spoons, reflect a new ideal of society, as the new elite could once again afford to support full-time specialists: warriors to enforce their rule and deter rivals, priests (perhaps Caesar's pan-tribal Druid caste) to provide divine sanction, architects to furnish them with palaces and citadels in the latest fashion, bards to eulogize their exploits and recite their genealogies and craftsmen to supply jewellery and adornments.

Early medieval accounts suggest that kings in pre-Christian, Celtic Ireland were invested with magical and supernatural powers and acted as intermediaries between their peoples and the gods. These kings had the power to bestow fertility on the land, a further indication of the links between political power and the control of agricultural production. While it is dangerous to make comparisons between societies widely separated in time and place, some such office of sacred, hereditary kingship may well have emerged in parts of Scotland by the around the first century AD. The footprint-carved stone in the causeway leading to the broch tower of Clickhimin in Shetland may be a rare Iron Age reflection of inauguration rituals still prevalent centuries later; most famously at Dunadd, the Dalriadic Scots capital in Argyll, where a similar carved stone was used in the initiation of kings within the hilltop citadel.

8
The clash with Rome

In AD 79 the Roman army, under Gnaeus Julius Agricola, governor of the Roman province of Britain, advanced into Scotland. Although this was to be the start of 300 or so years of contact, the Roman encounter with Scotland was ultimately little more than a series of military episodes, with periodic attempts at consolidation (see David Breeze's *Roman Scotland: Frontier Country* in this series).

The concerns of successive Roman emperors were generally focused firmly on the Mediterranean heartlands of the empire (**68**). Scotland, at the extreme north-western extent of their vast territories, was hardly central to their interests. Thus, while some emperors might make use of Scotland as a place in which to achieve relatively cheap military honours, when trouble arose elsewhere in the empire the northern frontier was a natural place from which to draw troops. Indeed, it was probably a combination of Scotland's peripheral geographical position and the inconsistency of approach by successive emperors that ultimately prevented full conquest.

68 The Roman Empire in the early second century AD.

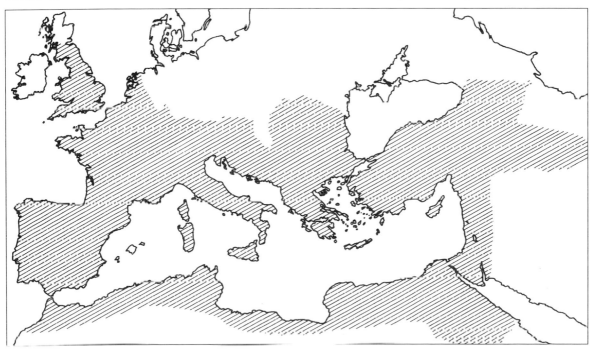

Scotland on the eve of invasion

The momentous events of AD 79 could have come as no great surprise to the Scottish tribes, since the power of Rome had been extending gradually but inexorably northwards for more than thirty years, ever since the Emperor Claudius' troops landed in the south of England in AD 43. Stories of Roman military prowess had probably been in circulation for even longer, at least since Caesar's conquest of Gaul, and attempted subjugation of southern England, a century earlier. Rome, then, had been a presence, however vaguely understood, in the social and political geography of the Scottish tribes for many generations.

It is possible that the kings and chiefs of Scottish tribes would have given asylum to displaced nobles, perhaps some related by marriage or alliance, who had fled their southern homes in the face of Roman expansion. As well as ousted leaders, the composition of refugee bands may plausibly have extended down the social hierarchy to include craftsmen, religious officials and warriors; all of those with a stake in the political and military fortunes of their masters. Farmers and others, whose living was more directly won from the land, are less likely to have fled northwards and there is certainly no evidence of anything approaching a folk migration from the south during the Roman conquest.

Before surveying the clash with Rome in more detail it is worth summarizing what we know of the indigenous peoples of Scotland in the years leading up to AD 79 by surveying the three best-studied parts of the country: the south-east; Fife and Tayside; and the Atlantic north and west.

The pre-Roman south

It used to be thought that the largest of the hilltop enclosures (those which extended to over 6ha (15 acres)), the so-called *minor oppida*, represented the capitals of the various Celtic tribes on the eve of the Roman invasion. Traprain Law was thus identified with the Votadini in Lothian, while Eildon Hill North was linked with their southern neighbours, the Selgovae.

The term *oppida* derives from the fortified proto-towns encountered by Caesar in Gaul during the first century BC and is also used to describe the sprawling and largely undefended settlements of the conquest period in the south and east of England. Whereas earlier hillforts were seemingly founded on the control of agricultural wealth, *oppida* capped a rather more complex social pyramid and were founded on the control of semi-industrialized craft production and trade. These sites seem to have been not only the seats of the southern Celtic aristocracy, but also centres of political, economic and religious authority; places where coinage was struck and where craftsmen worked.

In Scotland the largest hilltop enclosures were once thought to represent the northern equivalents of these southern centres; the culmination of the development of ever-larger hillforts during the Iron Age. However, as we have seen in chapter 4, the great majority of Scottish hillforts date to a rather earlier period, and the largest of them, such as Traprain Law and Eildon Hill, had their origins in the Bronze Age. The apparent absence of occupation attributable to the pre-Roman Iron Age on Eildon Hill North seems to preclude its identification as the Selgovae capital, even allowing for the limited extent of the recent excavations.

While a few large hillforts, such as the Dunion in Roxburghshire, seem to have continued in use, and even expanded to their greatest extent in the pre-Roman period, there is little to suggest that they functioned, like their continental counterparts, as proto-towns. The Scottish forts, so far as is known, had no specialist craft-working areas, no especially grand houses and no overtly religious buildings.

However, the one site that stands out from other Scottish forts is Traprain Law. Although the origins of occupation on the hill extend back at least to the Bronze Age, some activity clearly continued throughout the pre-Roman centuries. A few finds, such as small stone balls, probably

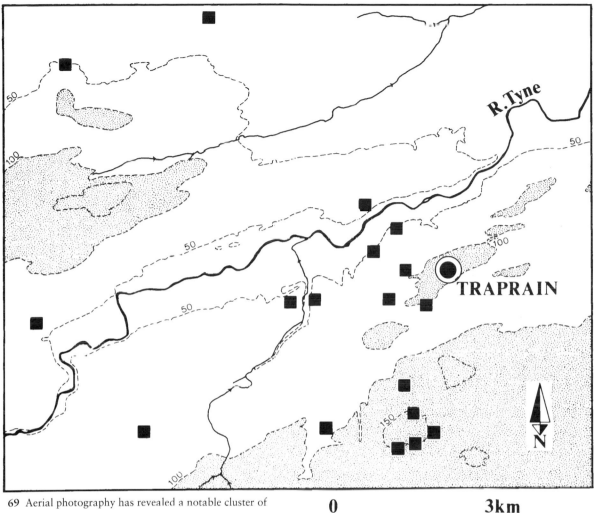

69 Aerial photography has revealed a notable cluster of rectilinear enclosures in the vicinity of Traprain Law.

used as gaming pieces, and scraps of pottery, may date to 400–200 BC, and there is evidence, from the excavated western plateau of the hill, of fragmentary ring-ditch houses that could be of similar date. While it is possible that the hill had become (or perhaps simply remained) primarily a place of sanctity where offerings were made and rituals practised, Traprain Law nonetheless remains the best, perhaps the only, candidate for a pre-Roman tribal 'capital' in the traditional sense.

Other likely settlements of the social elite have been identified in recent years. One of the most peculiar features of the buried archaeological landscapes revealed by aerial photography in

southern Scotland, for example, is the clustering of square and rectangular enclosures around (or more strictly to the south and west of) Traprain Law (**69**). The regular form of these enclosures, their low-lying and often ill-defended locations and a small number of radiocarbon dates from similar sites in Northumberland have led some scholars to believe that they were constructed under the influence of Roman fashions and represented the compounds of the Celtic elite during the occupation.

One such site recently excavated at Dalhousie Mains in Midlothian gives some credence to this idea. Radiocarbon dates suggest that the enclosure was indeed occupied during the first

103

70 Two examples of rectilinear enclosures, probably dating at least in part to the period of the Roman incursions: East Bearford in East Lothian (left) is unexcavated, but Dalhousie Mains (right) has produced radiocarbon dates for use in the first two centuries AD, although it may have been constructed a few centuries earlier.

or second centuries AD. However, the origins of the settlement seem to have lain rather earlier, in the last few centuries BC (70).

So, although any Roman influence on their form was probably indirect at best, the possibility remains that these enclosures were the homes of Celtic nobles, representing the abandonment of the overt militaristic associations of the earlier hillforts in favour of new fashions in keeping with more peaceful times. In this context, the cluster around Traprain Law may reflect the continuing importance of that area, even if the status of the hill itself remains something of a mystery.

In other areas local worthies were probably housed in unenclosed settlements, such as that at New Mains in East Lothian where high-status metalwork was discovered some years ago. Such settlements, lacking the cropmark-producing ditches of earlier enclosures, will always be hard to detect in the arable lowlands and many more may yet await discovery.

Whatever the disposition of the native elite in the south, however, the more modest settlements of the farming population are reasonably well known, at least in the uplands. Small lightly enclosed farmsteads, normally comprising from two to five small, stone-walled roundhouses (sometimes, perhaps misleadingly, called 'Votadinian' houses) with accompanying sunken yards, are found throughout the Borders and Northumberland, often lying among the remnants of contemporary fields and drove-ways (71). More recently, similar stone-walled houses have been found in the lowlands, notably in the latter stages of occupation at Broxmouth in East Lothian.

Although frequent discoveries of fragments of Roman pottery and other goods in these houses were once taken to suggest that they dated exclusively to the Roman period, recent radiocarbon dating has pointed to their origins in the last few centuries BC. Some of these stone-walled farmsteads appear to overlie earlier palisaded versions, and individual houses seem to have evolved, as at Broxmouth, from timber proto-types.

In some areas, particularly the Cheviots, these farms could be quite densely spaced, around forty being known in the Bowmont Valley alone, and their occurrence at altitudes of 350m (1150ft) and above shows the degree to which the Late Iron Age settlement expansion had penetrated into the uplands. Some of these settlements appear to be associated with cultivation terraces, presumably designed to prevent soil erosion from unstable hillslopes, which replaced earlier fields of cord rig (see chapter 5). The eradication of these narrow rigs, which had run up and down slopes, and their replacement by the new terraces must have been a considerable undertaking, and one in which whole communities presumably participated. Their ability to accomplish projects of this kind, together with the undefended nature of their farms, suggests that these upland communities enjoyed stable social and political conditions. Indeed, the new farms often, as at Hownam Rings, physically overlie the defences of earlier hillforts, as if to reinforce the irrelevance of the old social divisions.

North of the Forth

Beyond the Forth–Clyde isthmus rather different patterns of settlement seem to have prevailed. As in the south, the hillforts, always fewer in number, had been largely abandoned by the early centuries BC. Large hilltop enclosures such as the Brown Caterthun, and vitrified forts such as Finavon, both in Angus, seem to have lain unoccupied for some time, and perhaps the sole hint of high-status enclosed settlement in the first centuries BC or AD is a smith's workshop on the coastal fort of Cullykhan in Banffshire.

The main feature of settlement in this period, rather than hillforts or enclosures, seems to have been the unenclosed souterrain villages, particularly densely spread in Angus and southern Perthshire. The combination of these unprotected grain stores with the apparent absence of defensive settlement suggests that this area, too, enjoyed relatively stable conditions, in which agricultural produce was organized centrally and perhaps redistributed between different communities. The profusion of souterrains suggests that they were by no means

restricted to the seats of kings or tribal chiefs, although they may indicate the homes of locally important families, in which grain produce was accumulated from surrounding farms. There are a few rectilinear enclosures similar to those further south, but the lack of excavation prevents any real understanding of their likely status.

The cultural divide of earlier centuries, centred along the Forth or Tay, seems then to have been maintained during the immediately pre-Roman period.

The Atlantic north and west

To the north and west, in the Highlands and Islands, settlement was still dominated by Atlantic roundhouses. In Orkney and Caithness, power was wielded from broch villages such as Gurness and Howe. Elsewhere, a rather more fragmented pattern appears to have prevailed with dispersed farms, such as wheelhouses and complex roundhouses, dominating much of the Western Isles and Argyll, while isolated but locally impressive broch towers, like Mousa in Shetland, Dun Carloway in Lewis and Dun Dornadilla in Sutherland, may have housed local nobility.

Broch villages were clearly centres of power, but it is impossible to tell from their physical

71 The scooped settlement of Orchard Rig, Peeblesshire contains small, stone-walled houses typical of the early centuries AD.

remains alone just how far that power might have extended. One extraordinary written account, however, may cast some light on the nature of these pre-Roman societies of the north and west. A document written during the fourth century AD by the historian Eutropius mentions that Orkney submitted to Claudius at the time of his conquest of southern England in AD 43, more than a generation before Agricola's troops entered southern Scotland. Most archaeologists have dismissed this statement as a textual error, rather than face the possibility that an Orcadian king, remote from the mainstream of the southern Celtic world, could have been so *au fait* with the niceties of diplomatic manoeuvring.

However, Andrew Fitzpatrick has recently drawn attention to a find from early excavations at Gurness that might throw some light upon this question. Sherds found in the ruins of the Orcadian broch village quite clearly derive from a Roman amphora (a pottery storage vessel) of a type which had become obsolete by AD 60. This particular form of vessel seems to have been used as a container for the shipment of liqueur wine, either on its own or as a preservative for ripe olives. Roman goods of this period are notably absent further south, even at Traprain Law, which was to become a magnet for Roman goods during the occupation. Indeed the nearest examples of this particular amphora type come from Essex, more than 600 miles to the south.

Thus, some time prior to the Agricolan invasion, high-ranking Orcadians resident in Gurness had access to Mediterranean goods, while their southern neighbours apparently did not. It is tempting to suggest, as Fitzpatrick does, that the kings of Orkney had close links, perhaps through marriage or military alliance, with tribes far to the south, and were well aware of both the threats and opportunities for advancement that the Roman expansion created. Fitzpatrick has even suggested specific links between this Orcadian elite and contemporary tribes in Essex who submitted to Claudius at the same time.

How far the power of these Orcadian kings extended over the rest of the Atlantic north and

west in the first century AD remains a mystery. However, their repeated mentions in the classical literature, while the rest of the Atlantic zone is ignored, and the relative grandeur of Orcadian broch villages, combine to suggest that the kings of Orkney may have maintained some degree of control over their neighbours.

Any treaties that might have resulted from diplomatic contacts between Orkney and Rome were not to last. Although their geographical remoteness was to prevent any serious attempt at conquest, the Orcadian tribes were to feel the full force of Roman military might within just a few decades.

The attempt at conquest

Most of our knowledge of the first Roman advance into Scotland, during the reign of the Emperor Vespasian of the Flavian dynasty, comes from a biography of Agricola written by his son-in-law, Tacitus, an account seemingly based on the first-hand accounts of Agricola and his military colleagues. Although exasperatingly short on descriptions of peoples and places, this account is invaluable in setting out the basic story of these campaigns and the flavour of the times. The routes taken by the army can be traced in rather more detail from the remains of their marching-camps (72), built and abandoned as they moved.

After dealing with a native rising in north Wales and taking a grip on the administration of the province, Agricola's first season of campaigning in Scotland carried him as far north as the River Tay. The rapidity of the advance through the settled farmscapes of southern Scotland, together with the apparent absence of marching-camps and forts in well-populated areas such as East Lothian and Fife, has suggested to many scholars that Agricola had already secured the cooperation of certain southern tribes; notably the Votadini, whose territory included East Lothian and may have extended south as far as Northumberland, and the Venicones in Fife. It is also possible that Petillius Cerealis, Agricola's predecessor as

governor, may have campaigned briefly in the south-west of Scotland, perhaps smoothing Agricola's progress in that area.

It was common practice for Rome to ease its expansion by establishing client kingdoms along its frontiers (as has already been suggested for Orkney at the time of the Claudian invasion), so this scenario is by no means unlikely on the northern fringes of the empire. In some cases this might mean simply supporting an existing ruling dynasty against its internal rivals, and/or external enemies, while in others it might involve the installation of puppet rulers, perhaps drawn from the disaffected kin of the incumbent rulers. Indeed, Tacitus records that Agricola at one point considered invading Ireland, with the

72 Roman marching-camps, like this one at Dalginross, can help us chart the progress of the various advances into Scotland. The camp lies in the foreground and can be recognised by its thin enclosing ditch, rounded corners, and complex entrance half way along the side. The nearby modern buildings give some idea of the scale of the camp. To the top left lies Dalginross Roman fort; a smaller but more permanent and heavily-defended installation.

assistance of an exiled Irish prince, who presumably would have been rewarded with the throne of his native land.

It seems highly probable, then, that arrangements for mutual cooperation were concluded between Agricola and the Votadini prior to the Roman advance across the Forth and Tay, as no opposition from that quarter seems to have been either encountered or expected. It is perhaps not too far-fetched to imagine that relations between the Votadini and their northern neighbours were tense, and that the southern kings were happy to see their rivals quashed by a third party. The native resistance to Rome was, in no sense, a 'national' struggle.

Agricola's initial thrust across the Forth to the Tay was followed by the emplacement of a string of forts to block the Forth–Clyde isthmus. This effectively consolidated Roman control over the southern part of the country, although, as before, East Lothian and Fife seem to have been left ungarrisoned.

Subsequent assays took the army north through Strathmore, below the long-abandoned ruins of hilltop forts like Finavon, Barry Hill and the Caterthuns, and culminated in September AD 83 with the wholesale slaughter of the assembled Celtic tribes at the battle of Mons Graupius (the precise location of which remains hotly disputed). This Roman victory forms the finale of Tacitus' biography and was to mark the last major achievement of Agricola's tenure as governor. Even allowing for a little embellishment on the part of Tacitus (who claims that 10,000 Celts, a third of the force, were killed), this defeat must have been a serious blow to the Scottish tribes.

Not content with this rout, Agricola sent his navy to deliver a further pounding to coastal tribes as far north as Orkney in a further display of terrifying military superiority. The fact that Tacitus singles out Orkney for special mention implies that these islands were seen as a significant seat of native resistance and perhaps, as the archaeological evidence might suggest, the key power centre in the north of Scotland.

Despite his success, Agricola's tenure as governor ended shortly after Mons Graupius and he was recalled to Rome. His successor's name and achievements are unknown (since he had no Tacitus to immortalize him), but it seems that, within fewer than ten years, Agricola's northern forts had been abandoned. In the interim, a short-lived frontier system, comprising a close-spaced chain of timber towers and fortlets, flanking the road along the Gask Ridge west of Perth, had been built and abandoned.

The details of Roman policy in these years following Agricola continue to elude us, and we cannot know, for instance, how much the Roman withdrawal owed to native resistance and how much to imperial apathy and expediency. By the AD 120s, however, imperial policy had fixed the limits of the Roman Empire some distance to the south at a line demarcated by Hadrian's Wall, running through northern England.

Yet only twenty or so years later they were back. The new emperor, Antoninus Pius, seeking to earn some much-needed military prestige, struck northwards around AD 140 and embarked upon the construction of a new frontier. The Antonine Wall was a massive turf-built curtain drawn between the Forth and Clyde, bolstered by a series of forts, fortlets and smaller installations. A further line of forts ran north from the Wall as far as Bertha on the Tay, near modern Perth, while an infrastructure of roads and forts secured the newly annexed area to the south.

The Antonine network was apparently maintained until the army withdrew once again to Hadrian's Wall, around AD 165, and, despite the sporadically devastating effects of subsequent military adventures, represents the closest that the Roman Empire ever came to a lasting hold on southern Scotland (73 and 74).

The Celts under Rome

So, for around ten or twenty years towards the end of the first century AD and perhaps twenty-five years in the second, southern Scotland formed part of an empire, stretching south to Egypt, west to Portugal, and east to Mesopotamia (see 68). Within this enormous area certain groups of people had considerable mobility; for example, at the upper end of the scale, governors and lesser officials were posted far from their places of origin, and, at the lower end, auxiliary troops

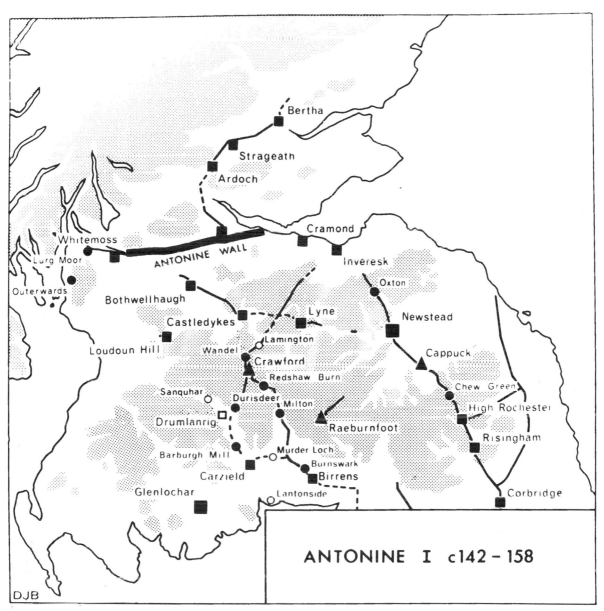

ANTONINE I c142-158

73 The Antonine frontier system.

were expected to serve wherever their units were needed. Exposure, however brief, to cultural influences, political systems and material goods from the Roman Empire surely cannot have failed to make some impact upon the ideologies and life-styles of the indigenous peoples of Scotland, at least in the south.

Yet the first impact of Rome was a military one, and, before assessing the legacy of Rome for the development of indigenous societies, we must first consider the repercussions of the initial clash.

The army on the march

We should not underestimate the disruption to the farmlands of lowland Scotland wrought by the passage of the Roman army which, during Agricola's campaigns, comprised some 25–30,000 men (75). Vast quantities of food, and other provisions such as firewood, would have been required to keep the army on the march and foraging off the land was common. In late summer this might mean harvesting

74 The Antonine Wall, seen here at Watling Lodge near Falkirk, carved up the native landscape.

75 The few contemporary depictions of the Scottish tribesmen inevitably present a rather biased picture of the encounter between Roman and native. This carving from the Bridgeness distance slab, found at the east end of the Antonine Wall, shows a typical celebration of the Roman victory.

growing crops from the surrounding fields, while in the early part of the campaigning season enemy settlements would have been raided for their stores of grain and other produce. Stock would have been at especially serious risk for communities along the line of Roman military movements.

It is highly probable, for example, that the campaign leading up to the battle of Mons Graupius would have seen the farms of Strathmore utterly devastated as the invading army passed along the valley, emptying the souterrains of their stored grain and pillaging the crops from the fields. Huge areas of arable and pasture land were commandeered for the erection of marching camps, up to 65ha (162 acres) in extent, some of which have been identified through aerial photography among the cropmarks of native settlements. The Agricolan fort at Cardean, in Angus, for example, seems to have been built on land deliberately cleared of indigenous settlement,

110

judging from the quantities of Iron Age pottery strewn around the site.

Famine, disease and depopulation would have followed for those areas directly affected by the passage of arms, areas like Tayside, the central belt, and the south-west; while even areas much further afield would have suffered, as those who would normally have been tending and harvesting crops were drawn from the land to fight. Doubtless the winter following Mons Graupius claimed many more victims than the battle itself.

Forts and frontiers

The Roman occupation brought with it major changes to the physical and political landscape of southern Scotland. Both in the Flavian period, beginning with Agricola, and under Antoninus Pius, integrated networks of forts, fortlets and watch-towers were set up to consolidate Rome's territorial gains (76). Complex road systems, complete with fords and bridges, carved the country up, enabling what must have seemed the miraculously swift appearance of military detachments wherever and whenever trouble arose.

The Antonine frontier itself would have been a major imposition on the landscape of southern Scotland (see 73 and 74). It demarcated the edge of the empire, and to cross it required the payment of dues, the surrender of weapons and adherence to specified times and points of access. Such restrictions on free movement would probably also have pertained in Flavian times, along the chain of timber towers and fortlets flanking the road along the Gask Ridge west of Perth.

It would be easy to exaggerate the impact of Roman military works. After all, indigenous communities had been modifying their environment quite drastically for thousands of years: the Cleaven Dyke in Perthshire, for example, built some 3000 years before the Roman invasion, cuts a swathe across the countryside for a distance of more than 2km (well over 1 mile); while the creation of lowland field systems and the upland forest clearances of the last few centuries BC were no less impressive cooperative projects that completely transformed the pre-existing landscape. Nonetheless, the scale and integration of Roman works was something quite new; almost inevitably it would have changed radically perceptions of what constituted social and political power for the indigenous communities of southern Scotland.

Social and economic life

While the imposition of frontiers and forts is relatively easy to demonstrate archaeologically, other impacts of the Roman occupation are less immediately obvious. During the periods of occupation the Roman army in Scotland was about 15,000 strong, and the taxes levied to support this number of economically unproductive individuals must have been a significant imposition on communities already disrupted by invasion. The Scottish tribes, lacking coinage, presumably paid their taxes in kind, most probably in grain or stock. However, other forms of payment, such as furs and hides, provision of labour or recruits for the auxiliary units of the Roman army, may have been equally acceptable. How such economic burdens would have affected traditional exchanges of labour, goods and patronage between social classes is unknown, but some disruption to indigenous institutions surely would have been inevitable.

The proximity of the empire would also have opened up a lucrative market for the slave trade. Although slavery probably already existed among the indigenous communities, the commercial aspects of the Roman slave trade may have encouraged an upsurge in raiding and warfare in the frontier zone, further destabilizing societies already weakened during the invasion.

Religion, too, would have been affected to some degree. The pan-tribal Druids of southern Britain and Gaul had lost their political influence; any organized priesthood in the frontier lands would have been a potential focus for resistance and thus an obvious target for suppression.

76 The Roman fort at Ardoch (the defences actually relate to three successive forts occupying the same site). The upstanding features shown here form part of an extensive complex which includes a large annexe, numerous temporary camps, a road, and a watch-tower. The various elements were in use at different times during the Roman period.

The impact of Rome, however, would have varied greatly across Scotland. While the Roman army would have prevented outbreaks of internecine warfare in the occupied areas, creating some stability, the southern tribes do not appear to have been assimilated into Roman provincial life to the same degree as their neighbours south of Hadrian's Wall.

Civilian settlements did develop around some of the larger forts in Scotland, notably Newstead, near Melrose, Inveresk, near Musselburgh, and Carriden, near Bo'ness. These satellite settlements or *vici* (singular *vicus*) seem to have served as local centres for craft production, industrial manufacture and trade and can perhaps be seen as proto-urban centres. Whether these settlements grew organically around the existing forts, or whether they were deliberately emplaced by the Roman military to serve the needs of the garrison, remains unclear. The known examples may be little more than glorified versions of the annexes attached to many other Roman forts, in which a range of ancillary functions was carried out. We also cannot tell whether they were populated exclusively by incomers or hangers-on, attached to the Roman garrison, or whether they included opportunistic members of the indigenous community.

Whatever their composition and origins, it does not seem that the *vici* had much influence on the surrounding rural communities, since Roman material of the first two centuries AD is scarce on native settlements, particularly in comparison with the superficially comparable situation on the broadly contemporary German frontier. The failure of any of the *vici* to survive beyond the Roman withdrawal seems also to suggest that they had little relevance to the indigenous people.

It seems unlikely, then, that much actual trade or exchange was carried out between the garrisons and their hosts. Rather, it appears that, within the occupied territories, the demands of the Roman army would have stifled economic production, destabilized social relations and humbled traditional leaders.

By contrast, in the ungarrisoned area of East Lothian (the fort and *vicus* of Inveresk lay on its westernmost extreme), the Votadini may have been allowed rather more leeway to maintain their way of life and social institutions, and indeed any tribute exacted by the Roman army may have been regarded as a price worth paying for the suppression of their troublesome neighbours. Whether we regard Traprain Law as a tribal capital or religious sanctuary, the rich array of Roman goods found there distinguish it from other native sites, and show that it continued to thrive throughout the first two centuries AD.

While Traprain Law is explicable in terms of its location in the heartland of the ungarrisoned East Lothian, the apparently similar site at Eildon Hill North in Roxburghshire is less easily understood. This hilltop settlement, which had apparently been abandoned since the Later Bronze Age (see chapter 4), was re-occupied during the first and second centuries AD, apparently at a time when the valley below was occupied by the Newstead Roman fort and *vicus*. Indeed, for a time at least, the hilltop itself was crowned by a Roman tower. It seems

inconceivable that the Roman army would have tolerated a fortified settlement so close to the fort, so we must presumably invoke some other explanation for the occurrence of hut platforms and Roman goods on the hilltop. Perhaps the hill was a religious site in the Roman period, or perhaps the occupation was confined to the periods when the Roman army had withdrawn further south. Without further excavation and much more precise dating, however, the site remains anomalous.

One other site which may have had a special status is Edinburgh's Castle Rock, although the medieval and later castle has obliterated most traces of the earlier settlement. Recent excavations on the rock have yielded higher densities of fine Roman pottery of the first and second centuries AD than have been found on any other native site apart from Traprain. A few centuries later, after the abandonment of Traprain Law, the Castle Rock was seemingly to emerge as the fortified capital of the kingdom of Gododdin, the post-Roman descendants of the Votadini.

While pro-Roman tribes such as the Votadini may have prospered, and while their more ambivalent neighbours may have stagnated under the oppressive presence of the Roman garrison, the tribes to the north of the Antonine Wall, beyond the permanently garrisoned zone, may have faced a rather different set of conditions. Frontier areas, like Stirlingshire, Perthshire and Angus, had been hit hard by Roman military operations from Agricola onwards, and would have been subsequently harried and subdued by border patrols. It is these areas, unshackled by the enforced passivity of the garrisoned tribes, but lacking the economic stability enjoyed by Rome's allies, that are most likely to have seen the breakdown of tribal institutions, economic crisis and the emergence of more fragmented and anarchic social conditions. These conditions may also have extended further north: the pollen record for Aberdeenshire, for example, shows that the earlier agricultural regime came virtually to a halt during the first century AD and was not to recover for several centuries.

Strife on the northern frontier was endemic, judging from numerous, albeit vague, written references to wars and military actions throughout the second century AD. However, the military exchanges between Rome and the local tribes went in both directions, particularly in the period after the construction of the Antonine Wall. Cassius Dio records a mass incursion from the north across the Roman frontier about AD 180. Around twenty years later, in stark contrast to the usual image of the Roman empire exacting tribute from its conquered subjects, Rome was forced to buy off one of the northern tribes, a people known as the Maeatae, to prevent further attacks and to obtain the release of prisoners. The Maeatae had not appeared in Ptolemy's list, and may have represented a new amalgamation of tribes in the troubled frontier zone. Place-names such as Dumyat and Myot Hill, in Stirlingshire, seem to place this group in the area just north of the Antonine Wall.

Another group frequently mentioned at this time are the Caledonians. Ptolemy's list of tribes, based on sources from the end of the first century AD, records the Caldones as a single tribe (see 50), seemingly occupying the Highland massif. However, the name was also apparently used in a looser sense, for example by Tacitus, to denote the lands and people north of the Forth or Tay. So, while by the latter part of the second century AD the Caledonians had become a major military force in the north, it is unclear whether they were a particularly dominant tribe, a new confederacy or whether the term was simply applied to any northern trouble-makers.

It was in such troubled frontier areas that an apparently alien settlement form seems to have been adopted: the lowland brochs (77). Unlike their more numerous northern counterparts, lowland brochs do not appear to have a local ancestry much before the first century AD. The handful of excavated sites have produced Roman pottery of first and second century AD date, as well as occasional fragments of Roman glass and metalwork. Indeed, in terms of access to Roman

material, the lowland brochs seem to have been among the richest settlements in southern Scotland, implying that the broch-dwellers were an important part of the native elite. Appearing as they do, however, in areas like Angus and Perthshire, where undefended open settlements had formerly sprawled across the lowlands, these grim, isolated structures seem redolent of a return to more stressful times and a more fragmented society. The broch at Hurly Hawkin and the stone-built 'duns' on Turin Hill re-occupy the sites of long-abandoned Angus hillforts.

Some scholars have seen these lowland brochs as the homes of opportunistic northern incomers, exploiting the power vacuum created by the defeat of the local tribes at Mons Graupius to stake their own land claims. It is not entirely clear, however, that lowland brochs and duns were a direct product of the Roman invasion. The brochs of Buchlyvie and Leckie in Stirlingshire, and Torwoodlee in Selkirkshire, for example, appear to overlie the remains of former timber roundhouses, suggesting that the settlements, if not the broch form, had at least some local pedigree. Indeed, it has been suggested that rather than representing the homes of incomers, lowland brochs represent simply the adoption of an exotic fashion, intended to display the status and prestige of the southern landed classes.

It seems unrealistic, however, to discount the importance of the wider political picture. Lowland brochs were probably built by local groups, since there is nothing else in the archaeological record to suggest an influx of bloodthirsty northerners. Yet the change in settlement pattern that they represent seems to reflect, to some degree, the breakdown in the pre-Roman economic patterns over much of lowland Scotland. That the excavated examples suggest that most of these brochs were abandoned, and deliberately dismantled before the end of the second century AD only serves to reinforce the wider picture of instability and social change that pervades the this period.

Whatever their origins, lowland brochs seem

to indicate some cultural influence from the far
north during the heyday of Orcadian broch
villages like Gurness, and the finest broch towers,
like Mousa. These northern lands, far beyond the
reach of routine military surveillance and frontier
policing, may have been substantially unaffected
by the Roman occupation of the south, at least
after their brief encounter with Agricola's navy
following Mons Graupius.

Septimius Severus

The aggressive actions of the Maeatae and
Caledonians seem to have caused disruption on

77 Edin's Hall in Berwickshire is one of the best preserved
of the lowland brochs. The broch itself is surrounded by a
substantial enclosure containing numerous stone-walled
roundhouses.

the northern frontier throughout the end of the
second and beginning of the third centuries AD.
As well as the sparse documentary references,
there is some archaeological evidence for the
destabilization of southern Scotland at around
this time. The signs of widespread settlement in
the Cheviots, for example, seem to disappear,
leaving what the archaeologist Peter Hill has

called 'tableaux of desertion', comparable to those left in the wake of the Highland Clearances of the nineteenth century. The final occupation deposits in the so-called Votadinian houses of the south-east often contain Roman pottery of first and second century AD date, but no later (although third-century pottery can be harder to identify), suggesting their possible abandonment in the violent decades following the Antonine withdrawal.

The last major Roman campaign in Scotland north of the Forth, ordered by the Emperor Severus in AD 210, seems to have been an attempt finally to stamp out the persistent threat from the north. It was directed against the Maeatae and Caledonians, who seem to have failed to keep to treaties only recently agreed with Rome. In response, Severus now proposed their extermination. The northern tribes by now knew better than to engage in open warfare and appear to have retreated to the hills, leaving the Roman army to gain its victory by burning crops, destroying farms and scattering what remained of the rural population (see **colour plate 13**).

This Roman victory, however, was never to be completed or consolidated. The death of Severus at York in AD 211, as he prepared to take personal charge of the second season's campaigning, finally ended Roman ambitions in the north. His son Caracalla seems soon to have embarked upon a measured retreat, negotiating treaties with the frontier tribes. This approach seems to have been effective in providing some measure of security for the Roman province, now firmly established behind the shelter of Hadrian's Wall, as there were to be no further reports of major problems on the northern frontier for three or four generations to come.

The Pictish wars

By the time we next hear of the northern tribes, almost a century later, they appear, at least to Roman eyes, to have coalesced into a new force, the Picts. The fourth century seems to have been characterized by repeated outbreaks of warfare, in which Rome appears often to have been on

the defensive; a reversal of the early Roman encounter with Scotland.

Thus, in AD 305 the Emperor Constantinius Chlorus campaigned against the Picts, as apparently did his successor, Constantine the Great, in AD 312, and his son, Constantine II, in AD 342, all apparently acting to repulse aggression from the north. In a further series of campaigns, culminating in AD 367, the Picts united not only with the Scots (the name probably refers, at this time, to people from Ulster), and the enigmatic Attacotti (whose origin is entirely unknown), but also with the Hibernians (from Ireland) and the distant Germans and Franks, in a concerted series of attacks on all sides of the Roman province. The Roman writer Ammianus Marcellinus reports that marauding Pictish war-bands reached as far south as the Roman town of London. Both the scale of the attack and the far-flung nature of the alliances between these anti-Roman forces suggest a new degree of organization among the formerly disparate northern tribes. This 'barbarian conspiracy' of AD 367 was finally repulsed by the Roman general Theodosius, but further wars in AD 382 and around AD 400 show that no lasting progress had been made.

Although throughout this period the northern frontier remained fixed on Hadrian's Wall, the area to the north was under the surveillance of scouts who, in AD 367, betrayed the Romans to their northern enemies and were disbanded. The tribes between the Tyne and Forth, such as the Votadini and Damnonii, however, appear to have remained either neutral or perhaps even actively pro-Roman. Certainly the Roman writers refer to the repeated incursions of troublesome Picts and Scots, yet never mention any aggression from the southern Scottish tribes who would, thus, probably have borne the brunt of the Pictish raids of the fourth century AD.

These troubled times may be reflected in the final flurry of activity at Traprain Law. A build-up of domestic debris, containing Roman Samian pottery of third or fourth century AD date, shows that Traprain continued to flourish as an occupied centre, even after the Severan withdrawal and throughout the fourth century AD. Several factors, however, suggest that the decades around AD 400 witnessed a crisis of such magnitude that it was to bring about the final end of Traprain Law as a tribal centre.

The first was the construction of a new enclosing rampart, some 3–4m (9–12ft) wide, with stone facings inside and out, built over the remains of former dwellings. On its own this might signify little more than the efforts of a new leadership to stamp its authority on the ancient hilltop, but other, broadly contemporary, events suggest that the new defences may have been intended to protect against the threat of impending physical attack, possibly associated with one of the wars mentioned in the Roman sources.

Also in the latter part of the fourth century AD, and possibly at the same time as the new rampart was built, an extraordinary collection of Roman silverware, including bowls, spoons, flagons, dishes and plates (78, and see **colour plate 15**), was cut up and buried in a pit, apparently below the floor of an abandoned house. It is far from clear how this material came into the hands of the Votadini. It was most likely a diplomatic gift from the Roman authorities in the south, or perhaps the result of trading contacts, although we cannot be sure that it did not represent booty from a successful raid. The motives behind its burial are equally mysterious. It is most usually suggested that the hoard was buried for security, although its dismembered state is perhaps more reminiscent of the ritual offerings of earlier centuries. Either explanation, however, would be consistent with a period of social stress and imminent conflict.

Perhaps the clinching factor, however, is the absence from Traprain Law of material post-dating the end of the fourth century AD. The absence of closely datable Roman material would, in itself, be explicable in terms of the increasing difficulties of maintaining contact, as the neighbouring Roman province crumbled. However, Traprain Law, previously a centre of bronze production, lacks evidence for later native bronzework, which would surely have been present had the site remained a Votadinian centre after AD 400; although a heavy silver chain of post-fourth-century date, found during quarrying operations, suggests that the site was at least visited in later centuries.

The abandonment of Traprain must have been an enormously significant event in the history of the Votadini. Yet it formed only a small part of a much wider series of changes that was to transform the political and cultural situation of the whole of Britain. For at the beginning of the fifth century AD, after a series of calamitous civil wars and internal disasters, Rome withdrew its remaining troops, and, by

78 Part of the hoard of Roman silverware buried on Traprain Law in the late fourth century AD.

around AD 410, Hadrian's Wall itself was abandoned. The province of Britain was effectively cut off from what remained of the Roman Empire.

New kingdoms

Throughout the Roman period the indigenous peoples of Scotland seem to have undergone a process of gradual amalgamation. As we have seen in chapter 6, Ptolemy's *Geography*, dating from the mid-second century AD, but based on slightly earlier sources, lists numerous tribes in Scotland, including twelve north of the Forth. By the end of the second century only two tribes are mentioned in this area, the Caledonians and the Maeatae, while Cassius Dio, writing in the early part of the third century AD, states of the Caledonians that 'the names of the others (northern Scottish tribes) have been included in these'. Even allowing for the imprecision of these sources, they do appear to reflect a significant coalescence of small tribal groups into larger confederacies.

By the fourth century AD these confederacies seem themselves to have merged into an even larger unit known as the Picts, the name deriving either from a Roman nickname ('painted people') or from the name they called themselves. A panegyric (or eulogy) of the Roman emperor Constantine in AD 310 mentions the 'Caledonians and other Picts', implying that the coalition was, at least initially, fairly loose.

By the middle of the millennium, the Pictish kingdom appears to have dominated Scotland north of the Forth and Clyde, with the exception of Argyll (79). This latter area was occupied by the kingdom of Dàl Riata, a group with strong Irish links (their leading dynasties identified Ulster as their place of origin), although probably descended mainly from the indigenous Iron Age peoples of Argyll.

Long after the end of the Roman period, echoes of the tribal origins of the Pictish kingdom remained, in the form of its numerous component provinces. Each of these had its own local aristocracy who retained some degree of

79 The post-Roman kingdoms of Britain.

autonomy. Irish sources refer to a 'king' of the Pictish province of Atholl as late as AD 739; presumably one of many petty potentates who owed allegiance to Oengus mac Fergusa, the Pictish high-king of the time, and one of the most powerful and successful of all known Pictish rulers. A much more detailed study of the establishment of Pictland and the other Early Historic kingdoms is provided in Sally Foster's *Picts, Gaels and Scots* in this series.

The four tribes south of the Forth, listed by Ptolemy, seem to have undergone rather lesser transformations. The kingdom of Gododdin had emerged from the Votadini, centred in Lothian, probably by the time of the final refortification of Traprain Law, around AD 400 (see 79). Their neighbours to the west, the kingdom of Strathclyde, seem likewise to have evolved from the Iron Age Damnonii, while the kingdom of Rheged, in the south-west, also had its Iron Age antecedents, probably including Ptolemy's Novantae. The other southern tribe mentioned by Ptolemy, the Selgovae, had no obvious post-Roman successors.

Close links seem to have existed in this period between these southern Scottish kingdoms and areas within the Roman province to the south. The post-Roman kings of Gwynedd, for example, traced their ancestry to Cunedda of the Gododdin, who was said to have helped the Welsh repulse raids from Ireland, some time before AD 400. Cultural contacts between the post-Roman Celtic kingdoms of Wales, Cumbria and southern Scotland were to survive until the territorial links between them were severed by Anglian expansion in the sixth and seventh centuries AD.

It has been suggested that the Latinized names of early kings, listed in the genealogies of Strathclyde and Gododdin, refer to individuals installed by Rome during the Pictish wars to help ward off the persistent attacks from the north. Such a view would help explain the exploits of Cunedda, since it seems unlikely that a war-leader of the Gododdin could have operated in fourth-century Wales without Roman sanction or invitation. It has even been claimed that one of the fourth-century kings, Patern Pasrut (Patern of the red cloak, or shirt) of the Gododdin, derived his name from the garment traditionally worn by client kings invested by Rome. However, if this were true, the colour should really have been purple, and, in any case, the evidence for this degree of Roman intervention in the affairs of the southern Scottish kingdoms is, at best, tenuous.

Nonetheless, the impact of the Roman presence should not be underestimated. It could be argued that it was the prolonged threat of conquest that precipitated the formation of the alliances and confederacies that were eventually formalized with the establishment of the Pictish kingdom. Similar processes seem to have occurred elsewhere; for example, among the tribes beyond the Roman frontier in Germany. Rome's persistent interference in the affairs of the northern tribes may also have been crucial in creating the sense of shared ethnicity and identity that made their subsequent cooperation possible. The Roman empire, however, appears to have contributed little to the social institutions, settlement forms or material culture of the Picts.

There was perhaps some rather more lasting Roman influence on the southern Scottish kingdoms. Strathclyde and Rheged, under the influence of Rome, seem to have adopted Christianity even before St Ninian's arrival at Whithorn, around AD 400, while the Roman writer Tertullian states that Christianity had reached beyond the limits of the Roman province in Britain by as early as AD 200 (although modern scholars have cast serious doubts on this statement). The Traprain treasure, likewise, shows that the leaders of the Gododdin had access to goods bearing Christian motifs, although the symbolism need not, of course, have been appreciated by its owners. A stone from Traprain, inscribed with the first four letters of the alphabet, seems to confirm, however, that some degree of literacy had percolated from the Roman south into southern Scotland prior to the abandonment of Traprain Law.

9
Epilogue

With the collapse of Roman control in southern Britain, new cultural forces began to exert an ever greater influence. Indeed, the spread of Anglo-Saxon languages and political control through the British Isles was, within a few centuries, to disrupt and marginalize Celtic-speaking societies to a far greater extent than the Roman empire ever did.

By the close of the sixth century AD, less than 200 years after the abandonment of Hadrian's Wall, the Anglian kingdoms of Deira and Bernicia had become the most powerful force in northern England, threatening the survival of the Celtic kingdoms of southern Scotland. The struggle between these powers was eloquently documented by the poet Aneirin in his *Y Gododdin*, an elegy for the warrior aristocracy of the Gododdin defeated at the Battle of Catraeth (probably Catterick in Yorkshire) around AD 600. This poem was apparently composed, shortly after the battle, at the Gododdin capital, Din Eidyn, although the earliest surviving manuscripts date from the thirteenth century. Despite the disaster of Catraeth, the Gododdin struggled on as a kingdom for a further generation until Din Eidyn itself fell to the Angles around AD 638.

Despite the disappearance of the kingdoms of Gododdin (and Rheged, a few decades earlier), and the growth of Anglian influence, the dominant powers in Scotland remained the Celtic-speaking Picts and Scots. By the ninth century AD, however, when these two groups merged to form the kingdom of Alba (later Scotland), Celtic-speaking societies persisted only on the northern and western fringes of Europe; Scotland, Ireland, Wales, Cornwall and Brittany. The histories of these later Celtic kingdoms and communities are beyond the scope of this book, but the formation of Alba is described in more detail in Sally Foster's *Picts, Gaels and Scots* in this series.

Celtic connections?

A great deal of historical and geographical distance separates these Early Historic kingdoms from the Iron Age *Celtae* or *Keltoi* known to Greek and Roman writers; so much, in fact, that the utility of any concept of a 'Celtic Europe' is open to considerable question.

The Celts were, after all, never a unified people. Even within Iron Age Scotland, itself just a small part of the Celtic-speaking world, we can recognize deep-rooted cultural boundaries: one perhaps dividing the tribes either side of the Forth and Tay; another separating the north-east tribes from those of the Atlantic north and west.

While the proximity of the Roman empire seems to have been a catalyst for the creation of new kingdoms and cultural identities, these did not require a recognition of any common 'Celticness'. Although the Celtic kingdoms of Strathclyde, Gododdin and Rheged seem to have recognized some kinship with their contemporaries in Cumbria and Wales (indeed

Y Gododdin only survived as a Welsh text), there seems to have been no such sense of identity with their Pictish neighbours. The Celtic languages spoken by the Scots of Dàl Riata and the Picts appear not even to have been mutually intelligible, given Adomnan's remark in his *Life of Columba* that the saint needed an interpreter during his sojourn at the court of the Pictish king Bridei in the sixth century AD. Such deep and long-lasting divisions seem to undermine any notion of a common Celtic identity.

Neither were Celtic-speaking societies static or timeless. It can be difficult to appreciate the duration, in human terms, of some of the historical processes that we have discussed. Assuming around twenty-five years for a generation, for example, the Picts who raided southern England in the 'barbarian conspiracy' of AD 367 would have included the great-great-great-great-grandchildren of the Maeatae and Caledonians who resisted Severus in AD 210; they themselves may in turn have been the great-great-great-grandchildren of the tribesmen who fought Agricola at Mons Graupius in AD 83. The period from 1000 BC to AD 500 saw the passing of some sixty generations. Even in innately conservative and rural societies, significant cultural and linguistic changes are inevitable over such protracted periods. Indeed, change, whether in society, material culture, religion, settlement or economy can be demonstrated throughout our whole period.

Despite all of these reservations, however, when we consider Scotland from a wider, European perspective, the concept of the Celts lies at the heart of some of the most important issues in prehistory. If the spread of Celtic languages can indeed be related to the cosmopolitan societies of the Later Bronze Age, then we must surely envisage a degree of linguistic unity over much of temperate Europe for almost the whole of the first millennium BC. If there was never a 'Celtic Europe', there was at least a 'Celtic-speaking Europe' from the Later Bronze Age, if not earlier.

While the centuries that followed saw the fragmentation of society, at least in northern and western Europe, certain aspects of material culture, such as hillforts and the spread of La Tène art, show continuing contacts. Did the links forged in the Later Bronze Age dictate that, although the complex Bronze Age networks of exchange may have broken down, common ideologies, cultures and languages ensured some similarities in subsequent social development? In Scotland, Iron Age contacts can be glimpsed only occasionally, for example through the occurrence of certain types of hillfort design, rare La Tène objects and the use of military techniques such as *chevaux-de-frise*. Yet even these intermittent indicators of contact, together with the documentary evidence for the presence of Celtic-speakers, demonstrate that the prehistory of Scotland can and should be understood in the context of the wider European scene.

The Celtic communities of Scotland who first enter written history in the first and second centuries AD were not, then, as was once thought, recent invaders from some continental Celtic heartland. Scotland was, as it had been for centuries, an intrinsic part of a Celtic-speaking Europe.

Places to visit

Museums

Many of the major finds relating to Celtic Scotland can be seen in the Museum of Scotland, Edinburgh (due to open in 1998).

Archaeological sites

Several Iron Age sites are in the care of the Secretary of State for Scotland and are looked after by Historic Scotland. These have on-site information and are probably the best sites to begin with. Following the coast clockwise from Shetland they are:

Clickhimin, broch and settlement, Shetland	HU 4643 4082
Jarlshof, broch and settlement, Shetland	HU 3980 0955
Mousa, broch, Shetland	HU 4573 2366
Ness of Burgi, fort (blockhouse), Shetland	HU 3878 0839
Gurness, broch, Orkney	HY 3818 2685
Grain, souterrain, Orkney	HY 4413 1161
Midhowe, broch, Orkney	HY 3716 3061
Rennibister, souterrain, Orkney	HY 3971 1259
Carn Liath, broch, Sutherland	NC 8704 0137
Dun Dornadilla, Sutherland	NC 4571 4500
Culsh, souterrain, Kincardineshire	NJ 5048 0548
Ardestie, souterrain, Angus	NO 5030 3444
Carlungie, souterrain, Angus	NO 5110 3597

The Caterthuns, forts, Angus	NO 5550 6690, 5480 6610
Tealing, souterrain, Angus	NO 4121 3816

Cairnpapple Hill, henge, West Lothian (not perhaps an Iron Age site, but there are a few graves in the henge that may be of this broad date and the site may have been held sacred in the Iron Age)   NS 9872 7173

Holyrood Park, City of Edinburgh (the park contains four forts and several settlements; the best guide is *Arthur's Seat and Holyrood Park: A Visitor's Guide*, by Caroline Wickham Jones, 1996, HMSO)   NT 27 73

The Chesters, Drem, fort, East Lothian	NT 5076 7826
Castlelaw, fort and souterrain, East Lothian	NT 2290 6385
Barsalloch Fort, Wigtownshire	NX 3472 4121
Rispain Camp, Wigtownshire	NX 4293 3993

Castlehill, Bar Hill, North Lanarkshire (a fort apparently overlain by the Antonine Wall)   NS 5255 7265

Torr a' Chaisteil, dun, Arran	NR 9219 2326
Dunadd, fort, Argyll	NR 8365 9356
Dun Beag, Struanmore, Skye	NG 3395 3861

Dun Telve, Glenelg, Lochalsh	NG 8290 1725	Traprain Law, fort, East Lothian	NT 5800 7470
Dun Troddan, Glenelg, Lochalsh	NG 8338 1723	North Berwick Law, fort, East Lothian	NT 5564 8422
Dun Carloway, Lewis	NB 1899 4122		

(these two sites are owned by the local authority and have interpretation boards and a visitor car park)

Aside from these examples, Iron Age sites can be found in all parts of Scotland and it would be impossible to list them all here. The best available guides are the *Exploring Scotland's Heritage* series, organized region by region, which feature good photographic coverage, site descriptions and advice on access for sites of all periods.

White Meldon, fort, Scottish Borders.	NT 2193 4283
Eildon Hill North, fort, Scottish Borders	NT 5545 3280

A few important sites not in state care are listed below. However, these are mostly on private land and you should seek permission before entering unless otherwise noted.

Burnswark Hill, fort, Dumfriesshire	NY 1860 7870
Ardifuar, ring fort, Kintyre	NR 7894 9692
Dun Ardtreck, Skye	NG 3350 3581

Kilphedir, broch and hut circles, Sutherland	NC 9943 1891

Dun Cuier, Barra	NF 6641 0340
Dun Scurrival, Barra	NF 6954 0810

Finavon, fort, Angus	NO 5065 5567
Barry Hill, fort, Angus	NO 2623 5038

Dun Vulan, South Uist	NF 7140 2980

Pitcur, souterrain, Perthshire	NO 2529 3738
Queen's View, homestead, Perthshire	NN 8631 6010

Loch na Berie, broch tower and Pictish settlement, Lewis	NB 1034 3516
Dun Bharabhat, Lewis	NB 0987 3530

Further reading

A list of other books in the Batsford/Historic Scotland series is printed on p. 128. Several will be of interest to readers of this volume.

Most published work on the Scottish Iron Age is in the form of academic papers in specialist journals. However, you may find some of the following books well worth reading.

Iron Age – general

Cunliffe, B. *Iron Age Communities in Britain*, Routledge, London 1991. A detailed and wide-ranging account.

Cunliffe, B. *Iron Age Britain*, Batsford, London, 1995. A general review.

Morrison, I. *Landscape with Lake Dwellings*, Edinburgh University Press, Edinburgh, 1985. A colourfully illustrated introduction to crannogs.

Piggott, S. *The Druids*, Penguin, London, 1968. Inevitably somewhat outdated given its publication date but still engrossing reading.

Stead, I. *Celtic Art*, British Museum, London, 1985. A good comprehensible introduction to a subject about which a great deal has been written.

Watson, W.J. *The Celtic Place-Names of Scotland*, Birlinn, Edinburgh, 1993. A modern edition of a classic work first published in 1916.

Iron Age – academic studies

Armit, I. (ed.) *Beyond the Brochs*, Edinburgh University Press, Edinburgh, 1990. A collection of papers bringing together recent work on Atlantic Scotland.

Champion, T.C. and Collis, J.R. (eds.) *The Iron Age in Britain and Ireland: Recent Trends*, JR Collis Publications, Sheffield, 1996. As its title suggests.

Hill, J.D. and Cumberpatch, C. (eds.) *Different Iron Ages*, British Archaeological Reports, Oxford, 1995. An exploration of recent archaeological thinking on the Iron Age.

Regional works

Each of the following texts contains a sizeable chunk of Iron Age material. Sadly, there are no comparable publications as yet for southern and eastern Scotland.

Armit, I. *The Archaeology of Skye and the Western Isles*, Edinburgh University Press, Edinburgh, 1996.

Renfrew, A.C. (ed.) *The Prehistory of Orkney*, Edinburgh University Press, Edinburgh, 1985.

Ritchie, J.N.G. (ed.) *The Archaeology of Argyll*, Edinburgh University Press, Edinburgh, 1997.

Glossary

Atlantic roundhouse Massive-walled dry-stone roundhouse, most common in the north and west, incorporating a range of simple and complex variants of which the best known are the broch towers.

ard an early form of plough that simply breaks, rather than turns the soil.

bi-vallate fort A fort defined by two ramparts and ditches.

blockhouse Massive rectangular or curving segment of dry-stone walling, usually blocking the approach to an islet or promontory and often incorporating features of broch architecture. Found predominantly in Shetland.

broch or broch tower Massive-walled dry-stone roundhouse of tower-like proportions, found mainly in the north and west, dating to the last centuries BC and first century AD.

broch architecture An assemblage of architectural traits including hollow-walled construction, scarcement ledges and intra-mural galleries, usually associated with brochs, but also found to some extent in blockhouses, promontory forts and hut circles.

chevaux-de-frise Stones or timber stakes set in the ground to impede access, for example to hinder a cavalry charge.

cists Grave pits lined with slabs and usually covered by a capstone, forming a stone box.

cord rig Cultivated land divided into narrow parallel strips. Apparently characteristic of prehistoric agriculture in the uplands.

crannog A partly or wholly artificial islet supporting a house.

dun Derived from a Gaelic place-name meaning 'fort', this term has become an ill-defined catch-all for small, stone-built houses or enclosures that fall outside the traditional definitions of broch architecture.

Hallstatt Archaeological name for the earlier part of the Iron Age, taken from a cemetery site in Austria.

hut circle The remains of a prehistoric roundhouse, commonly surviving as a ring-shaped bank.

La Tène Archaeological name for the later part of the Iron Age, taken from a site in Switzerland.

multi-vallate fort A fort defined by multiple ramparts and ditches.

oppidum A proto-town or large settlement, defended or undefended, with evidence for a range of specialist functions such as crafts, industry, religion and political control.

palisades Stout fences of close-spaced posts set in narrow trenches packed with stones.

pit alignment A boundary formed of large pits, sometimes accompanied by a bank.

scarcement A ledge projecting from the inner wall of a building, probably to help support a roof or floor.

souterrain A semi-underground linear or curving structure, possibly used to store grain and other produce. Found most commonly in eastern Scotland north of the Forth and in the north and west.

uni-vallate fort A fort defined by a single rampart and ditch.

wheelhouse An elaborate dry-stone roundhouse divided by stone piers resembling, in plan, the spokes of a wheel.

Index

The author

Ian Armit is an Inspector of Ancient Monuments with Historic Scotland. He has excavated extensively in Scotland, with particular emphasis on the Western Isles, and has written numerous books and articles on Scottish and north-west European archaeology. Dr Armit is a Fellow of the Society of Antiquaries of Scotland and a Member of the Institute of Field Archaeologists.

Series editor: Dr David J. Breeze
Chief Inspector of Ancient Monuments, Historic Scotland

Titles in the series

Periods
Scotland's First Settlers
Caroline Wickham-Jones
Neolithic and Bronze Age Scotland
P.J. Ashmore
Celtic Scotland
Ian Armit
Roman Scotland
David J. Breeze
Picts, Gaels and Scots
Sally Foster
Viking Scotland
Anna Ritchie
Medieval Scotland
Peter Yeoman
Fortress Scotland and the Jacobites
Chris Tabraham and Doreen Grove

Sites and subjects
Edinburgh Castle
Iain MacIvor
Iona
Anna Ritchie
Prehistoric Orkney
Anna Ritchie
Scotland's Castles
Chris Tabraham
Scottish Abbeys and Priories
Richard Fawcett
Stirling Castle
Richard Fawcett
Scottish Cathedrals
Richard Fawcett

Forthcoming
Ancient Shetland
Val Turner
Pilgrimage in Medieval Scotland
Peter Yeoman
Scotland's Historic Shipwrecks
Colin Martin